# Transformed by Grace
## Paul's View of Holiness in Romans 6-8

# Transformed by Grace
## Paul's View of Holiness in Romans 6-8

By J. Ayodeji Adewuya, Ph.D.

Cascade Books
A division of *Wipf & Stock Publishers*
199 West 8th Avenue, Suite 3 • Eugene OR 97401

Cascade Books
A division of Wipt & Stock Publishers
199 West 8th Avenue, Suite 3
Eugene, OR 97401


*Transformed by Grace*
*Paul's View of Holiness in Romans 6-8*
Copyright©2004 by J. Ayodeji Adewuya, Ph.D.
ISBN: 1-59244-800-3
Publication Date: September 2005

10     9     8     7     6     5     4     3     2     1

## Dedication

This book is dedicated to Pastor W. F. Kumuyi,
the General Superintendent of the Deeper Christian Life Ministry,
from whom I first learnt about *the way of holiness*.

# Preface

Every book has a story behind it. This book is a part of my Christian journey. It is a testimony about the power and possibilities of God's grace. I was born and raised as a Methodist and baptised as a young boy in the Salvation Army, two denominations that belong to the Wesleyan holiness tradition. Nevertheless, it was not until 1974, a year after my conversion, that I became exposed to an in-depth teaching on sanctification. While reading various books on the subject of holiness for personal edification, not only did the significance of Romans 6-8 in the teaching of sanctification become evident but also the discordant voices in its interpretation became louder. Chapter 7, it appears, has become a refuge for many believers who argue against the possibility of victory over sin in the present day. It seems that, on the one hand many scholars and commentators underestimate, unwittingly, both the power of and possibilities of grace while, on the other hand, they overrate the power of sin.

My pursuit of higher education heightened my passion for the subject of holiness and the significance of Romans 6-8, together with other crucial texts. When I joined the faculty of the Church of God Theological Seminary in 2001, I was given the privilege both to develop and to teach a course titled "Holiness in Paul." Not surprisingly, Romans 6-8 became a significant text to address. What is presented in this book is part of the broad picture of holiness in the Pauline corpus. It is my prayer and hope that God will use this book to stir up a passion for Himself and an insatiable craving to be Christlike.

# Table of Contents

# Acknowledgements

Putting this book together in its present form would have been more difficult without the help of various people, although the views expressed in it and whatever mistakes the reader may find there are entirely mine. I am grateful to the following people for taking time to read the book in its manuscript stage: my colleague at the Church of God Theological Seminary, Dr. Rickie Moore, Dr. Dean Fleming of the European Nazarene Bible College Switzerland, and Dr. Kent Brower of the Nazarene Theological College, Manchester. I am particularly grateful to Dr. David Root, the General Editor at Cascade Books for his encouragement and desire to see the work in print. My Graduate Assistant, Bill Powers deserves mention for his hard work in typing portions of the manuscript. Given my handwriting, it was a challenge.

# Chapter 1

## Introduction

*orisa, boo le gba mi, se mi boo se ba mi*
*god, if you cannot save or change me,*
*leave me as you met me*
*- An African (Yoruba) Devotee's Prayer*

The prayer above provides three valuable lessons that inform this writer's exploration of sanctification in Romans 6-8. First is the belief of the suppliant in the ability of the "god" to save. Second is the expectation that salvation brings an out-and-out change in circumstances in life. Third is that a salvation or deliverance of only a partial nature is not worth being labeled as such. In other words, salvation or deliverance, in accord with what the word means, must be to the uttermost (cp. Heb. 7:25). The foregoing is further buttressed by the African belief in God as "Oba tii gbani lagabatan," which means God is the "King who saves or delivers completely." Although many Christians would concede that sanctification is an important aspect of Christian life and experience, it has suffered both a serious neglect and gross misunderstanding. The unfamiliarity of many believers with the scriptural teaching on holiness has caused many to think of sanctification either as impossible of attainment or as something theological and theoretical—unrealisable in the present. Many seem content to think of sanctification as a doctrine to be believed rather than a quality of living to be demonstrated on a daily basis. One wonders whether such is not the result of unwillingness to meet the demands of holy living. But Christian sanctification cannot thus be neglected by those who want to understand the Christian gospel and who want to try to live in obedience to Christ. It relates to Christian duty. It has much to do with Christian happiness. And it ought to be foremost in Christian purpose. Beeke's comments are on target:

The call to holiness is, in a real sense, *wholistic*, for our whole life is involved—soul and body, time and eternity. It involves every sphere of life in which we are called to move: in privacy with God, in the confidentiality of our homes, in the competitiveness of our occupation or work, in the pleasures of social friendship, . . . .The call to holiness is a seven-a-day week, 365-day-a-year-call. It is radically compre-hensive; it belongs to the core of religious faith and practice.[1]

The Christian life ought to be an experience of growing victory over sin and of growing likeness to Christ, a goal that is ahead of us to challenge our strongest desire and effort.

## Romans: Influence and Message

The profound influence of the book of Romans on Christianity is well documented in Christian literature. St Augustine's "conversion," Martin Luther's Reformation, and John Wesley's Aldersgate experience are but a few of the most notable examples of people whose lives have been greatly impacted by the book.

Regardless of divergent opinions and scholarly debates concerning the purpose of Romans, it is hardly in doubt that Paul wrote as a pastor-theologian whose main goal was to nurture, encourage, and edify the members of the church to which he wrote. One of Paul's stated purposes was to go to Rome to "preach the gospel" (Rom. 1:15), a phrase that has often been narrowly understood in terms of evangelism, that is, the proclamation of the good news to sinners in an attempt to bring them to a saving knowledge of Christ. Thus, narrowly understood, evangelism is synonymous with soul-winning. However, for Paul, preaching the gospel means more than reaching the unsaved with the gospel. It includes instructions, exhortations and warnings. This explains why Paul desired to preach the gospel to the Romans who were already Christians. As such, for Paul, the proclamation of the gospel goes beyond the initial proclamation of the good news to include the exhortations and challenges to live a life that is worthy of the gospel, that is, a life that has been transformed by grace and manifests itself in the fruit of holiness. Paul does not separate community life and worship. Both are inseparable parts of wholesome and holy living. Moreover, in Pauline usage, to "evangelize" refers to the total task of the apostle in proclamation. . . . One cannot distinguish between missionary preaching and preaching addressed to the Church (cf. Rom. 1:15 with 15:20; Gal. 1:16,23)."[2]

The emphasis on the sinful condition of the human heart, and the possibility of transformation by grace and blamelessness of the personal life constitute much of the burden of Paul's writings. This is especially true of Romans. In the opening chapters of the book, Paul deals with the problem of sin as it relates to humanity. He begins the epistle with one of the most graphic pictures of sinful humanity found in the Scriptures. It is needful to look at this picture to see the kind of humanity that God's grace seeks to save and transform, in as much as God's remedy for sin will not become clear until the undone human condition is understood. Following the thematic statement in Rom. 1:16-17: "For I am not ashamed of the gospel, for it is the power of God for salvation to everyone who believes, to the Jew first and also to the Greek. For in it the righteousness of God is revealed from faith to faith; as it is written, 'But the righteous man shall live by faith'," Paul goes on to declare: "the wrath of God is revealed from heaven against all ungodliness and wickedness of men who by their wickedness suppress the truth" (Rom. 1:18). One must immediately ask, "what could have brought the wrath of a loving God upon his creatures?"

As Paul argues in the entire section of 3:1-20, and particularly in 1:18-32, the problem is sin. Paul maintains that sin, in whatever forms or shades, is not a laughing matter. Paul characterises sin as deliberate rebellion against God's truth and his revealed righteousness. Humanity began their downward plunge by not honoring God as God; "they became futile in their thinking and their senseless minds were darkened" (Rom. 1:21). In their willful disobedience "God gave them up in the lusts of their hearts to impurity"; "He gave them up to dishonorable passions"; He "gave them up to a base mind and to improper conduct" (Rom. 1:24, 26, 28). Paul's picture of the human situation, that is, of sin and its consequences is unmistakable. With a fine brush, in Romans 3:9-23, especially, Paul highlights the human dilemma, showing the horridness of sin as well as its universality. Humanity outside Christ, regardless of social status, gender, genealogy, or geography, creed or religion, stood condemned. And as Paul painstakingly argues, sin must be judged. Is there any hope for humanity? Paul would say, yes. As a result, Paul moves beyond the description of human plight and the hopeless situation into which sin has thrust humanity. He goes further to show the remedy. Specifically, Paul speaks of justification. God has made provision for forgiveness and reconciliation. Paul's emphasis on solidarity particularly in Rom. 1:16-3:20 is striking.

Paul obviously thinks of humanity in solidarity rather than humanity as individuals although the latter is not excluded. One must therefore grant the possibility that Paul understands justification of the ungodly to be relational and to involve a strong corporate nuance. The passage brings the Gentile and Jewish strands together—both are guilty; neither is righteous. Even though the Jews may be the only ones who recognize the Old Testament sources of the scriptures that Paul recites here, the metaphors are plain and powerful. Paul closes with a statement, which he will develop further, that the purpose of the Law is to make us aware of sin.

How can sinful humans establish relationship with God? Or, how do sinful humans become righteous? In theological terms, how does God justify the sinner and what does it mean? At various points in Romans 1-3 Paul has argued that God's righteousness is a gift from God conditioned upon acceptance by faith. He provides a detailed explanation in Rom. 3:21-26. First, God's righteousness is a gift to sinful humanity, by which he sets them right with Himself. Second, the gift of righteousness is to be received only through faith and not through any good works that humans may do (vv. 22, 28). Third, God's gift of righteousness abolishes the distinction between Jew and Gentile, not only because all alike have sinned and turned against God, but also because all alike can be and are to be accepted by faith alone (vv. 22, 23, 27-30). Fourth, God's gift of righteousness is available to humanity because of Christ's death. Lastly, the teaching on justification is found in the Old Testament but is clearly revealed in Christ (vv. 21, 25, 26). As the discourse continues, Paul continues to narrow the differences between his Gentile and Jewish listeners. He works through the fact that both groups have only one path to justification—through Christ (Rom. 3:21-4:25).

In Chapters 4-5, drawing on an aspect of the story of Abraham

# Introduction

substantiated with a quotation from the Psalms (Psa. 32:1-2), Paul presents the reader with an example of how God justifies the sinner. Because of human failure to attain to God's standard of righteousness God had to provide the way of salvation as illustrated in the life of Abraham whose "faith is reckoned as righteousness." "God reckons righteousness apart from works" (Rom. 4:5, 6). The only way to get right with God is by faith. Succinctly, Paul argues that (1) Abraham's righteousness came by faith, vv.1-5, (2) David's righteousness did not come from his own works, vv. 6-8, (3) Abraham's righteousness did not come from circumcision, vv. 9-12 and (4) Abraham's righteousness did not come as a result of his obedience to the law, vv. 13-17. As a minister once said, "We contribute nothing to our own salvation except the sin from which we are saved." And the gift of righteousness can be received only by faith (Eph. 2:8, 9; Titus 3:5). The story is told of how, in 1860, Charles Blondin four times walked across the Niagara Falls on a rope that stretched tightly from one side to the other. Once he pushed a wheelbarrow and at another time he carried a man on his back. Then he offered to carry across another man who was watching, but the man refused. "Do you believe that I can do it? asked Blondin. "Yes, I do," replied the man, "but I am not willing to try." Abraham's faith demonstrates that faith is more that simply believing about God or accepting what He says. It means and involves a reliance on Him and a deliberate commitment to Him.

In Romans 6-8 Paul focuses on the new life in Christ —its privileges and obligations. In reality, the three chapters constitute a unity. But the emphasis in chapter 7 centers chiefly on the conflict with sin and the law, while chapter 8 treats more definitely the realities of the new life in the Holy Spirit. In chapters 6 and 7, Paul answers the criticism that salvation by grace encourages sin (6:1-14), allows sin (6:15 to 7:6), and makes the law a sinful thing (7:7-25). In chapter 8, he shows how the Holy Spirit enables and energises the believer to live in a manner that the law could not match. To understand the challenge to holy living, which the conversion experience imposes on believers, it is necessary to study seriously the truth in these three chapters. This is the task to which we now turn.

## Chapter 2

## Free..... But! — Romans 6:1-23

It is early morning October, 1, 1960. Something of great importance has happened. A nation has been born and the vestiges of its colonial past have been removed. Instead of the Union Jack, a new flag of green-white green is unfurled. The signature tune of the British Broadcasting Corporation that was played every hour on the Nigerian Broadcasting Service is gone. "Free, free, at last!" the people shout. However, a relationship with the immediate past colonial master continues—a relationship that is now completely different from the form and the shape in which it previously existed. It is an entirely new situation. The new freedom comes with responsibilities. This is the situation one finds in Romans 6-8. Again, it is necessary to put the situation in its context.

Romans 1-5 describes both the human predicament and the ensuing freedom that comes as a result of Christ's death. A new era has dawned. Salvation is not just a possibility but a reality, and the Roman Christians to whom Paul writes were basking in their new-found freedom from their "old master", sin. After describing the results of life under grace in chapter 5 and how such a life of peace, exultation, and reconciliation is possible through the death of Christ, Paul now proceeds to quell any notion that life under grace means license to sin. Instead, he shows in chapter 6 that because of the believer's new status–that of being identified with Christ in his death and resurrection (vv. 1-14), and that of becoming a slave to Christ and righteousness (vv. 15-23)–the Christian is now able and is expected to live a life of holiness.

In Romans 6, one faces important questions such as: How does sin relate to the believer? If an end has been made to morality—morality that is not grounded on Christ's sacrifice, and grace alone is effectual, why not go ahead, then, with sinning? If, after all, it does not depend on our own actions, what does it matter how we live? What are the implications of justification? What are we to do with our new freedom in Christ? Paul answers these questions in three ways, which divide the chapter into three natural sections, viz., 6:1-11; 12-14; 15-23. In the first section, Paul considers the believers' new situation, that is, the indicatives, using concepts such as "died to sin" (6:2), "baptized into Christ" (6:3a), "baptized into his death" (6:3b), "buried with Him through baptism" (6:4), "our old self crucified so that the body of sin might be destroyed" (v. 6), and "died with Christ" (v. 8). Specifically, in this section Paul draws out the implications of the believers' faith-union with Christ, the outward expression of which was baptism. In these verses Paul was not saying what Christians *ought to* be like; he was simply describing what Christians are *like.* Our first responsibility, Paul would conclude in this section, is to understand the facts of who we are in Christ upon conversion and baptism.

In the second section, Paul, drawing on the indicatives, challenges the believers not just to take some specific actions but to become in life what they are in Christ, that is, to live up to the reality of their new existence as part of God's holy people. Our duty is to live the kind of life that is suitable for the kind of people we now are. Third, Paul uses the slavery metaphor to show the absurdity of the believer's remaining under the control of sin. The believer's life is described both as a life of freedom and slavery simultaneously. Paul's overriding concern here is ethical. Instead of offering a theoretical explanation of the believers' relation to sin, he focuses on the experienced fact of sinning, indeed, of living a sinful life. He is about to show the incompatibility of sin with the new life in Christ (grace). Sin and grace are shown to be mutually exclusive. His intention is to lead the Roman Christians to the realization that the gospel of grace, rightly understood and properly interpreted, leads not to licentiousness (far from it!) but to righteousness.

## A. The Believer's New Situation - The Indicatives (Romans 6:1-11)

1. What shall we say then? Are we to continue in sin that grace might increase? 2. May it never be! How shall we who died to sin still live in it? 3. Or do you not know that all of us who have been baptized into Christ Jesus have been baptized into His death? 4. Therefore we have been buried with Him through baptism into death, in order that as Christ was raised from the dead through

the glory of the Father, so we too might walk in newness of life. 5. For if we have become united with Him in the likeness of His death, certainly we shall be also in the likeness of His resurrection, 6. knowing this, that our old self was crucified with Him, that our body of sin might be done away with, that we should no longer be slaves to sin; 7. for he who has died is freed from sin. 8. Now if we have died with Christ, we believe that we shall also live with Him, 9. knowing that Christ, having been raised from the dead, is never to die again; death no longer is master over Him. 10. For the death that He died, He died to sin, once for all; but the life that He lives, He lives to God. 11. Even so consider yourselves to be dead to sin, but alive to God in Christ Jesus.

## 1. The Believer's Union with Christ—Dying to Sin

The question in verse 1 follows directly on Paul's assertion that, "where sin abounds, grace much more abounds" (5:20). The criticism that Paul's teaching on justification by faith and salvation by grace encourages sin results from complete misunderstanding of what salvation is, what grace is, and what faith in Christ does to one's life. To partake or share in the grace of Christ means to partake of his life. And where Christ is, sin must take to its heels. Grace does not encourage sin; it rather encourages righteousness. It is a dynamic compulsion to a new way of living, as will be argued here. This is the fundamental premise to the rest of this section.

In v. 2., Paul opens with his characteristic emphatic answer ("never," "may it never be," "impossible "),[3] followed by the question, "how shall we who died to sin continue to live in it?" The fundamental premise of the Apostle's thought and argument in this section is that believers have *died to sin*. The main question to be answered is: what does it mean, or stated differently, to what concrete or specific reality does it point in the life of the believer? In providing an answer to this crucial question, Paul expresses his answer by the use of various indicative concepts that describe the Christ-event. Needless to say, by its nature the indicative mood generally expresses facts. Paul is therefore using the various indicative concepts, such as *died to sin* to assert without equivocation the *fact* that believers have died to sin.[4]

In the history of interpretation, this concept has been interpreted and understood in various ways, the most common of which is the forensic or juridical interpretation. Interpreted this way, the concept *died to sin* means that God in a legal way has made a declarative judgment that those who are "in Christ" have died to sin. To die to sin means that Christians have died in God's judgment with respect to sin simply because God counts the death of Christ to be theirs. Usually, the concept of justification by faith, to which this passage obviously alludes, becomes a forensic formula and suggests no more than a sterile, objective acquittal, or, as some scholars rightly assert, a legal fiction. Hence, *died to sin* does not refer to or involve a definite and personal experience in the life of the believer. This interpretation is very unlikely in the light of Paul's appeal to the Roman Christians' common knowledge in the verses that follow, especially that of baptism in v. 3f. which suggests an experiential reality. Furthermore, the second question, "how shall we live in it?" goes against a juridical interpretation of this verse. The question stands in contrast to the concept *died to sin*. As such, this question cannot be rightly or properly interpreted and understood except the answer be found on the existential or experiential level. This being the case, it is clear that the antithesis *died to sin* would probably have been understood by the recipients of this letter in the same way. It should be understood experientially. Paul must have had a definite, momentous experience in mind when he wrote to the Roman Christians that they *died to sin*.

A careful reading of Rom. 6:1-11 reveals that the phrase *died to sin* occurs three times in this short paragraph. It is twice applied to Christians (vv. 2, 11) and once to Christ. These words show what Paul was about to explain, namely, the freedom that the believer has —freedom from sin. Without doubt, this is a crucial matter for anyone who wants to live as a Christian, but many Christians have found it difficult to comprehend. As a starting point in the interpretation of this phrase, it is useful and necessary to find an explanation for this phrase by first looking at Christ's death to sin. The believer's death to sin will then be interpreted within the context of Christ's death. The indisputable fact is that Christ's death was experiential, though it should be clearly understood that there is a distinction between Christ's death and the believer's. When Christ died on the cross, it was more than a physical death. It was a death in relationship to sin, a spiritual separation from His Father (cf. Rom. 6:10). The important thing to note is that when Christ died for our sin, he died to the sin; he was done with it. When then did the believer die to sin? Paul says we died to sin when we were baptized in connection with his death (v. 3). Also, in v. 7 Paul says, "we died with Christ." This verse enables us to talk about the believer's participation in Christ's death as well as his dying along with Christ. The believer died to sin when Christ died. In his use of dative "to sin" which could be understood as "in reference to sin," Paul forcefully asserts that as far as sin is concerned, the believer is dead. It signifies that the power of sin has been broken for the new person in Christ. This is "union with Christ." However, as maintained so far, there is a corresponding experiential reality in the believer's life. The relative pronoun *hoi tines*, (literal translation: "such people as we") is used deliberately here with a qualitative nuance to suggest the meaning "we who are of such nature that," pointing to an ethical decision. It further suggests that Paul identified himself with the experience he was writing about. Having stated the basic fact upon which his refutation of the rhetorical question in v. 1. rests, that is, the believer's death to sin, Paul now moves on in the following verses to explain how believers have died as well as to state the implications of that dying.

## 2. A Lesson from Baptism (vv. 3-5)

3. Or do you not know that all of us who have been baptized into Christ Jesus have been baptized into His death? 4. Therefore we have been buried with Him through baptism into death, in order that as Christ was raised from the dead through the glory of the Father, so we too might walk in newness of life. 5. For if we have become united with Him in the likeness of His death, certainly we shall be also in the likeness of His resurrection.

Paul continues his explication of the phrase *died to sin* in v. 2 by making a reference to baptism, which he evidently assumes that his readers are familiar with. The keyword in this verse is *baptism*. There are different views on its usage here. The significant thing to note is that, in most cases, when Paul refers to baptism, the primary reference is to water baptism (cf. 1 Cor. 1:13-17; 12:13; 15:29; Gal. 26-28; Eph. 4:5). Furthermore, by the time the epistle was written, the word *baptize* in its usage had virtually become a technical expression of the rite of water baptism. It seems to be extremely misleading to speak of baptism as a mere metaphor for Spirit-baptism.[5] Therefore, *baptism* here is better understood as a reference to water baptism.[6]

Paul uses baptism to illustrate the point and to teach a very important truth about Christian experience. When he says that we "were baptized into Jesus Christ" and "were baptized into his death," he means that we were baptized "in relation to Christ" and "in relation to his death." Our baptism declares our union with him in connection with his death; that is, we have faith in his atonement for sins. "We are buried with him by baptism into death," by which we declare that we have died to sin; and "as Christ was raised up from the dead by the glory of the Father," we declare by baptism that we have experienced a spiritual resurrection by the power of God. We thus pledge to walk in newness of life. Baptism is a pictorial representation of spiritual regeneration. It declares personal faith in Jesus Christ, who died and was buried and rose again from the dead. Baptism represents the believer's confession of having died to sin and of having been raised up spiritually to a new life.

In verse 4, Paul draws a conclusion from the preceding argument and proceeds from the act of dying to the fact of death. Paul probably alludes to burial, because it is common knowledge that it presupposes that death has already occurred. Baptism dramatizes and makes objective the death to sin which has already occurred at the Cross.[7] When are believers buried with Christ? To this question it is probably right to refer back to vv. 2-3. We died to sin when we were baptized into his death, that is, provisionally on Golgotha and experientially at conversion, to which baptism is an attestation. The baptism into death is so that we should be resurrected with him to walk in the newness of life. The conditional clause *"so that we may walk in the newness of life,"* refers us to the raising of Christ from the dead. The possibility of walking in the newness of life is linked with the resurrection of Christ. There must therefore be a present sense in our rising with Christ. Though the Christian is not yet fully sharing in the risen life of Christ as suggested in the future tenses in vv. 5 and 8, he or she stands clearly upon the positive side of the "death-life" water-shed. Furthermore "walking in the newness of life" is an appropriate and pointed contrast to the question "shall we live in it (sin)?" in v. 2. Both statements refer to a life-style or continued existence. Resurrection with Christ is the underlying consideration. It seems, therefore, that more basic than the thesis that the believer has died to sin is the notion of union with Christ in the various phases of his messianic experience. Paul's line of reasoning may be outlined as follows: on the one hand, as Christ died (to sin, cf. v. 10), so believers by virtue of union with him in his death have died (to sin, cf. v. 2); on the other hand, as Christ was raised from the dead (cf. v. 4), so believers by virtue of union with him in his resurrection have been raised to a newness of life (v. 4.). Thus, because of the solidarity between Christ and believers, the inseparability of resurrection from death in the case of the former means the inseparability of resurrection from death in the experience of the latter.

From the foregoing, it seems clear that, in v. 4c, Paul views the resurrection with Christ not only in terms of solidarity with him at the time-point of his resurrection but also as part of a decisively new situation in the life of believers, who have now become part of God's holy people.[8] Paul's repeated stress is that death with Christ (to sin and to the law) includes an experiential aspect which excludes the possibility of continuing in the bondage and practice of sin. Accordingly, resurrection with Christ likewise involves an existential component. This new situation is called by Paul, "walking in the newness of life," and it is the present dimension of the believer's "resurrection" with Christ. "Walking" in this phrase is to be understood in an ethical sense. The "new person" in Christ has the ethical and moral responsibility as well as the empowerment to live a holy life. Christ's resurrection has been presented not to indulge the readers in dreams of future glory, but to exhort them to moral resolution here and now.

### 3. Union with Christ - A Fact in Experience (vv. 5-11)

As we have seen, baptism is meant to declare a fact in Christian experience. That fact is spiritual union with Christ. In conversion there has been a death to sin and an experience of new life within the heart. This is a new kind of life. It has new moral quality and new moral powers. It is on this ground that Christian sanctification is the expected result of justification by faith or regeneration through the power of God's Spirit. In all these verses the apostle emphasizes in the strongest way that the Christian is one with Christ in death and resurrection. Death and resurrection cannot really be separated. If our death to sin is real, resurrection to newness of life is also real—in fact, it is normal. The old self was actually put to death that the body marked by sin should be made of no effect or put out of operation.

Paul's words mean that there is reality in the experience of conversion. We have experienced something that causes us to hate sin. The whole moral nature has been changed at its source. If repentance is real, one has changed his or her mind about God and Christ and also about sin and utterly turned from it. If faith in Christ is real, he or she has committed him or herself to a new Lord. If conversion is real, the Christian has in his or her inner being the living Christ. All this is a part of the reality of union with Christ which ought to issue forth in Christ-like living. A radical change takes place in conversion. It is a once-for-all experience. Christ died once, and death no longer has dominion over him. He died for sin once for all, and so his relation to sin came to an end when he gave his life for sin; and now he lives in an eternal relationship with God. The Christian has experienced the benefits of Christ's death, which made possible redemption from sin; and now the believer enjoys the benefits of Christ's resurrection in that he or she has the power of the living Christ to effect sanctification in his or her life. On this basis Paul later says, "Reckon also yourselves to be dead indeed unto sin, but alive unto God through Jesus Christ our Lord." We are to live in keeping with the fact of Christian experience, the fact of spiritual regeneration, the fact of union with Christ having been established by faith and being continued by faith and being fruitful for the ends of sanctification. Grace is more than absolution from sin; it is a dynamic antidote for sin. It never encourages to sin; it constrains one to hate sin and flee from it.

Verse 5 goes on to explain further vv. 2-4. Here Paul explains the link established in v. 4 between the resurrection of Christ and the believer's walk in the newness of life. Undoubtedly, the underlying thought is again the inseparable connection of Christ's death and resurrection. The inference to be drawn from such connection is that if we are united with Christ in his death we shall be also in his resurrection. Disjunction in our case is as impossible as disjunction in his.[9] Contrary to some scholarly opinions, it seems very obvious that in Rom. 6 "dying and rising with Christ" is not presented by Paul as a motif expressing the process of transformation or gradual conformity to Christ. Rather the unmistakable and sustained emphasis of Paul is on the definitive breach with sin which lies in the believer's past. The believer has died to sin. It is significant to note the already and the not yet of the believers' union with Christ here. While in verse 4 Paul alludes to the believers' resurrection as a present reality, in verses 5 and 8 it is cast in the future.

In verses 6 and following, Paul restates and amplifies the preceding facts about the believers' death with Christ in vv. 4a and 5a.[10] Paul begins by asserting that "our old self has been crucified with him." The major difficulty in the interpretation of this phrase is the identification of the old self and the reality to which his crucifixion points. The meaning of the "old self" is a much debated issue among New Testament scholars and commentators. It has sometimes been understood as a simple reference to the unregenerate person, that is, a person in the unconverted state. Another view of the old self, namely that which sees it as a reference to the old nature, has been rejected by most scholars, because it looks too much like anthropological dualism—rather like Dr. Jekyll and Mr. Hyde. This is a psychological interpretation which seeks to attribute sin in the life of the believer to the old self. Taking this view results in the tendency to see the believer as being made up of both the old self and new self. To equate the terms "old self/new self" with nature goes beyond acceptable evidence. They are never used psychologically at all. They are historical.[11] Other writers and commentators have suggested that the term "old self" ought to be understood in a sense that is denotes more than a mere "unregenerate selfish person." Instead, to such writers, the term "old self" is related to the basic depravity of human nature. Thus, the old self is understood as a description of the unregenerate person in his/her entirety, that is, the whole of our fallen human nature—the whole self in its fallenness, in contrast to the new person in his/her entirety.[12] In recent scholarship, it has been suggested that the terms old self and new self are to be understood as a reference to humanity in general in its relationship with Christ. In other words, the terms are to be interpreted in a corporate sense. Hence, Paul is talking about that which once took place in Christ and in which his people had a part in Him in a corporate sense.[13] Such is the confusion that surrounds the understanding of the phrase. Unfortunately still, lexicographers throw little light on the proper interpretation of the meaning of the "old self."[14]

What then is the "old self"? The passage itself offers some solutions. The first is to give a due recognition to the context in which the phrase occurs. What do we learn from the context of the verse? As noted above in the introduction to the exegesis of this passage, Paul's ultimate concern is ethical. This is why he has described the believers' situation with indicative phrases, such as "died to sin", "baptized into Christ and his death," "buried with Him" (vv. 1-8) of which the old self being crucified is an intricate part. These indicatives are a list of factual statements[15] about what Paul says had happened to the believers when they put their faith in Christ and, as a result, entered into a relationship with Christ. Actuality is implied; that is, what things Paul says happened are deemed to be true. On the basis of these statements, Paul was about to motivate them to live holy lives. In this verse Paul shows that the result of the crucifixion of the old self is that we should no longer be slaves to sin. When does this take place in Christian experience? As regards the specific moment when this takes place in Christian experience, Paul points in the present context to the believer's faith-union relationship with Christ which is expressed in baptism. The old self died when the believer died to sin and was resurrected in Christ to become a new man in status and experience. This suggests that the "old self" must therefore have been crucified at the time the believers were delivered from the bondage of sin. Existentially, this was at conversion or baptism.

The second solution in identifying the "old self" is the examination of the antithesis to the "old self," which is, the "new self." Usually, the "new self" is also identified with the time one enters into Christ. Based on this, it is right to suggest that the phrase "old self" should be interpreted as "the man we once were," and not just the selfishness of the believer which was crucified. Further, an examination of the word "crucifixion" as used by Paul helps us in identifying the "old self" as well as the reality to which his crucifixion points. Looking at some other passages where Paul employs the language of crucifixion (Gal. 2:20; 5:24; 6:14.), we may note that Paul never uses this word as metaphor for self-denial, but instead, always and consistently relates it to the death of Christ, denoting the manner of death Christ died. At the same time he uses it as a synonym for death (with Christ).[16]

Therefore, it is obvious that, speaking of the "old self" having been crucified (having died) with Christ in Rom. 6:6, Paul is referring to the sinner dying with Christ to sin,[17] which is the same as the old self having died (having been crucified with Christ) provisionally on the cross in the death of Christ and experientially when the believer puts his faith in Christ. If the question be asked concerning the finite point in time when this takes place, the answer we maintain is at conversion (-baptism).

In the next clause, Paul expands the purpose of the crucifixion of the old self. It was "in order that the body of sin might be destroyed or rendered inoperative, so that we may no longer serve sin" The participation of our old self in the crucifixion of Christ is to lead to the rendering inoperative of "the body of sin." The "body of sin" has also been understood in various ways. Basically, there have been three ways of explaining its meaning. The first is to understand the word in its strict sense, as a reference to the physical body, so far as it is an instrument in the service of sin.[18] Others explain the usage of the word in this particular context figuratively. The body of sin therefore denotes sin as a heavy mass or as an organism or system of evil dispositions. Paul's usage is therefore not to be viewed in real anthropological terms.[19] There is no lexical support for this usage. Thirdly, the body is equated with the whole person in respect to the person's ability to control him or herself and be the object of his or her own action, in which case the physical body is not only relegated to the background, but completely excluded from Paul's use of the word *soma*. It seems appropriate, however, taking cognizance of vv. 12-13 where Paul uses the term in a parallel manner to the whole person, to interpret the word more broadly. The phrase should not be limited as a reference to just the physical body with an inherent principle of sin in it. Paul never portrays the body as necessarily and essentially sinful, though existentially it is. Rather it is viewed as amoral, that is, neutral. The choice of *soma* by Paul is probably intended to underscore the fact that the body is the instrument that we use in the service of sin by virtue of our solidarity with Adam.

When Paul says that the body of sin may be destroyed he is simply saying that sin's power is now broken and thus it is no longer sin's body. Because the "old self" was condemned and put to death in Christ's death on the cross, the flesh, the old mode of existence of sin, has lost its dominion and control over those who are in him. The concluding clause "that we may no longer serve sin" may be taken either as a result or purpose.

However, taking into consideration the imperatives that follow later from v. 12, the former seems more preferable. It will thus serve as one of the grounds for the imperative. As such, the verse anticipates the imperatives. In verse 7, Paul moves on to illustrate his theological point by reference to a general truth[20] for "he who died has been freed from sin." Paul's purpose is not to prove v. 6 but to illustrate his theological point by reference to a general truth. Verse 8 expresses Paul's certain belief that death to sin is followed by new life. As said earlier, "shall. . . .live" does not refer exclusively to future resurrection, but rather to participation in the resurrection life of Christ here and now. As we shared his death, so we share his new life. Verse 9 goes on to express the certitude conveyed in the preceding verse. The believers' confidence or assurance that he/she shares in Christ's resurrection life rests on the knowledge that Christ is alive forevermore. Verse 10 is a confirmation of the fact of Christ's endless life. Death has no further claim on Him. Christians' first duty is to understand who they are in Christ and live up to it.[21] This is the import of v. 11.

The argument in the preceding pages may be summed up as follows. First, the central thesis of this passage is that believers have died to sin. In establishing this, Paul based his argument on the believers' union with Christ, as well as upon their participation in the various phases of Christ's messianic work. When did this dying to sin take place? If believers died with Christ, the time can only be when Christ Himself died. However, such reasoning grasps only half the matter. This union, which is described with the various indicative phrases as I have attempted to show and maintain, is experiential in nature.

## B. The Imperatives - A Moral Obligation (vv. 12-14)

12. Therefore do not let sin reign in your mortal body that you should obey its lusts, 13. and do not go on presenting the members of your body to sin as instruments of unrighteousness; but present yourselves to God as those alive from the dead, and your members as instruments of righteousness to God. 14. For sin shall not be master over you, for you are not under law, but under grace.

What Paul has said, showing that sanctification is the rightful expectation of regeneration, in no way lessens the personal responsibility and moral obligation with respect to goodness. As Paul shows in verse 12-14, holiness of life is possible because one has become a Christian, but it is not an automatic result of conversion. The Christian must not only realise the obligation but choose what is good, to follow after righteousness, to strive for moral excellence. This is the implication of Paul's strong prohibition that believers should neither let sin reign in their bodies nor yield to the desires of the flesh. But there is more. The aorist imperative suggests that Paul has in mind a decisive, momentary action by the believers.[22] They were to present their members once and for all. Wesleyans refer to this as a *crisis* experience. Consequently, the physical body (made up of several members) should never be given over to the works of unrighteousness resulting in sin. Instead, believers must yield themselves to God and make every capacity of the body an instrument of righteousness in keeping with His purpose. Paul lays the responsibility at the believers' door. They are able to make a total yielding to God because they are already "alive from the dead." Here we find the dialectic nature of sanctification in the sense that the instantaneous and progressive are both required and held together in balance.

It is imperative that the Christian take God's side in the fight against sin and unrighteousness. The believer must recognize his or her own moral responsibility, practicing self-control and dedicating all energies to doing the will of God. Paul's imperative is followed by a sweet assurance: "Sin shall not have dominion over you: for you are not under the law, but under grace." What a promise, what an encouragement! A Christian—a regenerated person—is no longer under the dominion of sin. Sin's power has been broken by the redemption of Christ. We are not, therefore, helpless victims of sinful desire within ourselves or of sinful assaults from without. We can gain a victory over sin, not because of the law forbidding it, but through the power of grace by which we have been saved. The compulsions of grace are those of inner spiritual power and spiritual gratitude. There is inner aversion to sin, moral energy to resist sin, and constraining motivation to please the holy God.

### C. Free but Enslaved - Paul's Use of the Slavery Metaphor in Romans 6:15-23

15. What then? Shall we sin because we are not under law but under grace? May it never be! 16. Do you not know that when

you present yourselves to someone as slaves for obedience, you are slaves of the one whom you obey, either of sin resulting in death, or of obedience resulting in righteousness? 17. But thanks be to God that though you were slaves of sin, you became obedient from the heart to that form of teaching to which you were committed, 18. and having been freed from sin, you became slaves of righteousness. 19. I am speaking in human terms because of the weakness of your flesh. For just as you presented your members as slaves to impurity and to lawlessness, resulting in further lawlessness, so now present your members as slaves to righteousness, resulting in sanctification. 20. For when you were slaves of sin, you were free in regard to righteousness. 21. Therefore what benefit were you then deriving from the things of which you are now ashamed? For the outcome of those things is death. 22. But now having been freed from sin and enslaved to God, you derive your benefit, resulting in sanctification, and the outcome, eternal life. 23. For the wages of sin is death, but the free gift of God is eternal life in Christ Jesus our Lord.

So far, based on the discussion of 6:1-14, it could be concluded that Christian sanctification has its prospect, first of all, in the initial experience of conversion. The Christian has a new heart, and therefore is expected to live the life of a new person in Christ. The motivations for living on this level are inward and spiritual. Such is the thought Paul now develops in the next part of his letter. The paragraph begins with the same argument as in verse 1, in a slightly different form of words suggested by verse 14. Paul precedes his arguments in both sections (1-14 and 15-23) with a similar rhetorical question (cf. v. 1. and v. 15): "shall we live in sin because we are under God's grace" (v. 1–"so that grace may increase") and answers each time in the same way: "May it never be." The person who is "under grace" is the person who shares the life of Christ. The same succession of the indicative and imperative moods that characterized vv. 1-14 can be found in vv. 15-23, the indicative stating facts about the believers' changed status and the imperative giving what the believer must then do in light of his/her new position in Christ.

Again the objection to justification by faith or salvation by grace is faced: the contention that salvation on this basis allows sin. "God forbid," says Paul. This is never the case. The first point in Paul's argument is found in v. 16 where he states the commonly accepted fact that one is a slave of the one he/she obeys. Paul speaks about "putting oneself at someone else's disposal." Paul wants to make it clear that the real master is the one to whom one gives obedience and not the one to whom one pays lip service. Paul's use of "either...or" is a lively and emphatic way of stating exclusive alternatives, showing that one or the other must be chosen. Commentators have often cited Luke 16:13— "No servant can serve two masters; for either he will hate the one and love the other, or else he will be devoted one and despise the other. You cannot serve God and wealth," here as capturing best what Paul is trying to say. There are only two masters– "sin" or "obedience" (in this verse); whichever one of them that is obeyed is the real master. Sin in this and the following verses is personified as a power exercising effective rule over people.

The very opposite is true. We are not under law, but this does not provide an excuse for sin. Law does not motivate sanctification, but grace does. Paul now uses two illustrations, the first of which is slavery. A slave serves one master. No one can serve two masters. A person is therefore a slave of that to which he or she gives obedience or that which he or she recognizes as his or her master. The two alternative masters here involved are sin and righteousness. The Christian has made his or her choice. Once he or she was the slave of sin. Having acknowledged sin as master, the sinner lived according to the ways of sin. But that has now passed. A decisive change has taken place. Sin has been renounced as master and the believer has chosen righteousness. Could anyone ever doubt that this is the essence of repentance? It is a renunciation of the way of sin and a turning to the way of righteousness with such contrition of heart and earnestness of purpose that it means a genuine about-face. No person can choose Christ as Saviour without choosing righteousness as his or her goal. He or she thus commits him or herself as a slave of righteousness.

In verses 17-18 (cp. vv. 20-22), Paul makes his second point: that though believers were slaves to sin before (imperfect tense is used), they have now become obedient (aorist tense) to the "form of teaching which you have received" (v. 17) and have become slaves (again in the aorist) of righteousness (v. 18) and of God (the word for slave is an aorist participle,

v. 22). There is a clear transfer of authority here–from the power of sin to the power of God and his righteousness. The language of manumission is present—"having been freed from sin" (vv. 18 and 22), showing that the believer is no longer in bondage to his former master, sin. Paul, however, is not thinking of absolute freedom where the believer can do what he/she wants (the main teaching of the chapter). Life under grace is life under God, a life of righteousness and obedience. The apostle breaks out in thanksgiving: "God be thanked" for that great life-changing experience on the part of Christians. They have heard the way of salvation and learned about a new way of living. They have believed it, accepted it, and committed themselves to it. Thus they have "obeyed from the heart" the doctrine of salvation by grace and a radically new concept of morality and spiritual living. Paul is declaring that a Christian is not free to sin but set free from sin, not only in the sense that he or she is forgiven, but also in the sense that he or she has become a servant of righteousness.

Contrary to Dodd's assertion, in verse 18, Paul has not slipped to "sub-Christian" thought[23] when he claims the believer is enslaved "to righteousness," rather than "to God." In order to give all the more impact to his declaration that the Christian is not to sin because he is under grace, Paul expresses the new slavery in terms, not of the new master—God (as he does in verse 22), but in terms of the character of the new master. It would be amiss to suggest that he is using "righteousness" as a synonym for God. He is emphasizing that to be enslaved to God is to be enslaved to one whose character is that of righteousness and in whose kingdom sin has no legitimate role. Paul, from a theological standpoint, can affirm that the Christian is enslaved to righteousness because Christ Jesus has become, for the Christians' benefit, the embodiment of God's righteousness (1 Cor. 1.30) and because the Christian is united with Christ through the baptismal death and renewal of life. Consequently in union with Christ the believer is within the dominion of God's righteousness (cf. 2 Cor. 5.21).

Although the believer has been enslaved through union with Christ to God's righteousness or to God, there still remains the necessity—as the Corinthians had all too clearly demonstrated—of coming to be like the one to whom they are enslaved. Enslavement does not of itself bring submission and even submission may not transform one's personal character, regardless of how restrictive or oppressive enslavement may be. For Paul, transformation of personal character requires the positive co-operation of the subjected one. The people who have been enslaved must now present their members to their new master in an active volitional endorsement and acceptance of their new status, so that they may become those who reflect in their character the character of their owner. Paul's awareness of this need is reflected by his use of the aorist imperative in verse 19b. As those who are enslaved to God—not to sin—the believers must begin doing that which they have not previously done: they must present their members as slaves to God and his righteousness, the consequence of which will be their own personal sanctification and, ultimately, eternal life (verses 19b, 22). Once again, in a similar fashion to v.13, Paul calls for a decisive action by the belivers.

The motivation for Christian sanctification, therefore, is inward. The law is now written on the heart and in the mind (Heb. 10:16). Allegiance to a new master, whose ways are purity and uprightness and justice and love, becomes a constraining incentive for a new way of living. Paul does not emphasize it at this point, but the background of his thinking is the centrality and supremacy of Jesus Christ. A Christian is not a slave of righteousness in the abstract. It is a commanding moral ideal, a divine standard, but it is much more. This righteousness is related to Christ, found in Him, motivated by Him, exemplified by Him, and sought after in response to His lordship and in order to please Him.

Having laid the basis for holy living, Paul now gives in v. 19 his main point and he does this through a command. This command is similar to v. 13, but instead of using the phrase " do not go on presenting the members of your body to sin as instruments of unrighteousness," he substitutes the word "instrument" or "tool" for "slave." A tool connotes a more impersonal and passive adherence while "slave" connotes a more personal one, although both have the sense of being completely at the disposal of the owner or user. The use of the aorist tense not only suggests a definite action at a point in time but also implies a "wholehearted commitment" or, in Dodd's words, "a life deeply and irrevocably committed." The slave was something without value, a thing to be bought and sold generally. A slave belonged wholly to his/her master. A repeated element in vv. 15-23 is the concept of dominion, in terms of ownership not just domination. The slave was required to do his or her master's will to the fullest extent of his or her abilities and wholly to serve his or her master's interests. The division between the demands of the sin nature and that of righteousness is therefore made clear in the strong terms "slaves of sin" or "slaves of righteousness."

Another difference with v. 13 is that, whereas in v. 13 there are two commands, in v. 19 there is only one command (the positive one), and the negative aspect is used as a point of comparison to show how believers, now as servants of God, should place the members of their body in complete disposal to righteousness in the same way that before they had placed the members of their body in complete disposal to impurity and lawlessness. Therefore, instead of a lifestyle that results in lawless deeds, theirs will be a lifestyle characterized by holiness. Paul seems almost to apologize in verse 19.[24] The first part of the verse is an apology for using so much human terminology to describe a relationship that could not be described in just anthropological terms. The believer is not just God's servant; he is also God's son (Rom. 8:14-17), and this makes the analogy imperfect. Nevertheless, Paul used imperfect imagery to make his point: believers, as a result of being justified by faith, now belong to a new master, God and righteousness, and are therefore bound to put themselves under His disposal rather than under their former master, sin. Verse 19b posits that the believers had previously given themselves[25] over to be slaves to uncleanness and lawlessness. In using the aorist form of the verb *parístēmi* Paul evidently was recalling the entire manner of life in which these people once lived (constative aorist). He does not imply that now they do such; he does not use the perfect tense. It is quite significant that he uses the active voice: not "you were enslaved to...," but "you presented...as slaves..." In other words, Paul attributes to the believers the responsibility for what they have previously done, from which he infers that they can be charged with the responsibility presently to follow a new life-style.

In verse 19c Paul repeats himself (except for changing the indicative to the imperative) in the clause "...present your members as slaves..." in the context of a contrast with verse 19b. What stood as a previously realized fact provides the legitimation for Paul's appeal. Those who are now new persons who have experienced the death of the old self and are living, not under law, but under grace (verse 14) must begin presenting themselves as slaves to righteousness, just as those who were under law presented themselves as slaves to sin. But, it must be observed, Paul has just asserted in verse 18 that "you were made slaves to righteousness" (an aorist passive). Paul understood the weakness of human nature and knew the necessity for Christians to find true freedom through voluntary submission to the ideals and practices of righteousness. He makes a vigorous appeal to Christians by reminding them of the contrast between the old life and the new. The unregenerate person yields to uncleanness. His or her moral insight is faulty. His or her moral inclinations are corrupt. His or her moral resistance is weak. The result is filthiness and lawlessness. But the new life in Christ is set in a different direction. It is an instantaneous act, followed by a life process of consecration. In the old life, when we were servants of sin, we did not recognize the obligation to righteousness or respond to the demand for purity, truth and love. The result was a kind of conduct of which we are now ashamed. It may have included pride and unbelief, or it may have included covetousness, lying, and adultery, or it may have included drunkenness, violence, and profanity. For all the works of the flesh the Christian will be genuinely ashamed. The end of all these things is death. The life in sin is a state of death now and leads to eternal death and torment forever. What Paul is trying to help us to see is that, having been set free from sin, we have become servants of God, and the fruit or outcome of the Christian life is sanctification, "and the end everlasting life." Sin always pays off in death. The wages are always paid. It is a matter of receiving just compensation for one's deeds. But over against that, in striking contrast, God's free gift is "eternal life through Jesus Christ our Lord." This is not a matter of payment or of desert or of earning; it is a gift of divine grace. It is the priceless gift from heaven. It is a new kind of life in its source, in its power, in its quality, and in its destiny. It is a kind of life that can bear the fruit of sanctification, the fruit of the Holy Spirit—even "love, joy, peace, longsuffering, gentleness, goodness, faith, meekness, temperance" (Gal. 5:22-23).

The law demanded obedience, but grace supplies the power to obey. Therefore grace breaks the mastery of sin as the law could not. Paul now gives the ethical application of 5:12-21. When we were in Adam, we were under slavery to sin. Sin, as master, demanded shameful living (lusts, v. 12; unrighteousness, v. 13; lawlessness, v. 19; shameful things, v. 21). In Christ we can be slaves of righteousness which demands, in grace, virtuous living–sanctification (v. 19, 22). Justification has demands as did the law, but grace supplies the power to fulfill the demands and break the mastery of sin as the law could not. Paul illustrates this with the slavery metaphor.

In this chapter Paul has consistently spoken of the believers' status prior to their conversion as "slaves of sin." In these passages, although Paul does not explicitly formulate the notion of "sin" in such a fashion, it nevertheless has essentially been personified. One can live in sin, just as one can live in Christ (6:2). Sin may possess and reign in the body (6:6, 12, 13, 16-18, 20, 22). One may live "to sin" (6:11). One either receives the wage of death from sin (6:23a) or the free gift of eternal life from God (6:23b). No persons are free; none is his own master. All serve either sin or God. In verse 19, however, Paul says the former slavery was "...to uncleanness and lawlessness...," rather than to sin. Rom.1:24; Gal. 5:19, and Eph. 4:19 give reason to suggest that "uncleanness" is not so much the designation of that to which one was enslaved, as it is the summary term denoting the outward manifestation of the antecedent enslavement to sin, the power. While living in bondage to sin, one's deportment is characterized by uncleanness and lawlessness. The consequence of such life is that one becomes what one has done. If one has lived in lawlessness, one has become by that life the personification of lawlessness.

It is important to remember that it is to people whom Paul describes as "slaves of righteousness" that he speaks words of ethical exhortation. More precisely, he exhorts Christians who are enslaved to God or righteousness to submit themselves to God, rather than sin (cf. Rom. 6 and 12). Paul clearly saw the Christian as one who had–within the framework of his being enslaved to God–freedom either to obey or not to obey the master. Consequently, there was need for exhortation. Such freedom he does not explicitly or implicitly attribute to the one enslaved to sin. For that person there were no alternatives. The one enslaved to sin yielded himself to sinful life; the only consequence was sin. When the believers regularly commit themselves as slaves to God and his righteousness, the result will be that their behavioral patterns will begin changing. Their former lifestyle of enslavement to sin was bringing (verse 21) only things of which they could now be ashamed. Their new lifestyle of conscious submission to God and his righteousness will bring in its wake the gradual ethical transformation of the persons, of which they need not be ashamed. This transformation is the process of sanctification, of being made holy. This new life in which the person is experiencing his personal sanctification comes into being through the Christian's continuing to accept the reality that he is dead to sin's enslavement (cf. 6:11a) and that he is alive as a slave of God (cf. 6:11b), together with his continued keeping himself or his members within the dominion of Christ Jesus his Lord and the Holy Spirit (cf. Rom. 8:4, 5b, 10). Sanctification, the emerging fruit of the Christian's submission to God (cf. 6:22), is the process of becoming like Christ Jesus through whom the believer's transferal out of the dominion of sin has occurred (cf. 6:1-11), in whom the believer's transmutation into a "new creation" has occurred (cf.2 Cor. 5:17), and through whose "in-working" (together with that of the Holy Spirit) the believer's new life is being manifested (cf. Gal. 2:20; Rom. 8:11).

At this juncture, some observations about comments made in the literature regarding *hagiasmos* are necessary. Peterson's definition of sanctification in this context as "a dedicated state" rather than a progressive ethical renewal[26] is inappropriate. That is a quite acceptable definition of *hagiadzein*, as in 1 Cor. 1:2; 6.11; and Rom. 15.16 as those contexts suggest. However, it seems obvious that, in the present context (Rom. 6.19, 22), the persons whom Paul addressed are those who are *already* set apart for God's use. Rather than using the image of being set apart to God, in Rom. 6, Paul has used the image of being enslaved to God. The two amount essentially to the same thing. Consequently his exhortation in Rom. 6.19b is that those who died to sin's dominion and who began to walk in newness of life as God's slaves should live in conformity to God's character, as made known through Christ Jesus, not that they should be his possession. Robertson[27] and Denney[28] may be correct in emphasizing the ingressive nature of this process of sanctification, in view of the verbal idea inherent in *hagiasmos*. 1 Corinthians. 1:30, by contrast, illustrates that may denote a state of being rather than a process of development. This might provide a basis for interpreting *hagiasmos* as a state which shall be realized in the future.[29] Consequently it may be suggested that the phrase *eis hagiasmos* in itself does not indicate whether Paul means in verse 22 that "you are having fruit unto a state of holiness" or "…unto a process of becoming holy." Denney's observation that process and state have no meaning apart[30] is surely pertinent.

Verses 20-22 further contrast the life in slavery to sin and the life under the dominion of God. In v. 20 Paul describes the life under sin as free "in regard to righteousness." In reference to righteousness, those who are slaves of sin are free (not bound), meaning that they are not under any compulsion to do what is right. This kind of lifestyle, however, has no fruit but shame and eventually death. The meaning of "death" here is ambiguous but probably has a comprehensive sense, referring to physical as well as spiritual death, which will eventually culminate in eternal death. On the other hand, the fruit of slavery to God is holiness—both as a state and a process.

To summarize, it is clear from the preceding passages that those who have been justified by faith are no longer slaves to sin which leads to death. They have been freed from its power and are now servants of God and of righteousness. Since this is their position in Christ, they are commanded experientially to become who they are by placing themselves and the members of their bodies completely under the disposal of their new master, an obedience that will result in life. The evil character of the antinomian concerns Paul deeply, to the point of spending much time and space to correct the issue. He has clearly stated, expanded and illustrated why antinomianism cannot be accepted as a way of life for the Christian. He has shown the reader that the power of sin has been broken by death, and the purchase price has been met by the work of Christ on the Cross. Therefore, righteousness is expected of the Christian. A slave to righteousness is one who is a servant of the Lord doing His will, practicing His righteousness. And, the slave is one who finds freedom in his or her service because of his or her position in sharing the death of Christ. They have exchanged death for life everlasting.

# Chapter 3

## Not By the Law—Romans 7:1-25

In his foreword to James Fraser's *A Treatise on Sanctification*,[31] Sinclair Ferguson highlights the problem that surrounds the interpretation of Romans 7. Writing on Alexander Whyte of Edinburgh, he says:

> He had a standing arrangement with his bookseller that whenever a new commentary on the Letter appeared, it should be sent to him on a sale-or-return basis. Whyte's habit was immediately to open the new work and read through the author's comments on Romans 7:14-25. If the work did not view the passage as an exposition of Paul's *Christian* experience, Whyte simply re-wrapped it and returned it with a note to the effect, 'This is not the commentary for me'.[32]

Whyte's attitude is typical of many scholars and commentators with regards to the chapter.[33] Romans 7, particularly verses 14-25, has been an exegetical battleground within the church since the time of the church fathers. And it still is. The controversy concerns whether the struggle with sin, which Paul discusses in v.14-25, describes pertains to persons still unconverted persons or applies to Christians. Augustine wavered on the point, believing first that it applied to the unconverted, but later being persuaded it applied to believers. So, the passage continues to be used to defend the possibility of remaining a "sinning Christian." Interpreters and commentators have consistently gone to Romans 7 asking the wrong questions. No wonder they come up with the wrong answers. Recently, a popular radio preacher, commenting on Romans 7 said, "Perhaps the classic example of a sinning believer is the apostle Paul." Does this statement truly reflect what Paul is saying in Romans 7? Probably not. How then should one proceed? Perhaps a better way to go is to give more weight than has usually been done to the interpretation of Romans 7 in its wider context, particularly Chapters 6 and 8. In doing so we might be able to reach an interpretation of the passage that more accurately reflects not only Paul's teaching on holiness, both in the context of Romans and his other writings, but echoes that of other New Testament writers.

Beginning from Rom. 5, Paul describes the Christian's new situation by explaining how Christ put an end to the reign of sin and death (5:12-21). This is followed by his assertion that believers have died to sin—they are free and no longer under the law but under grace (6:1-14), and therefore must walk in the newness of life. The slavery metaphor was further employed to affirm the believers' freedom. Those who have been justified by faith are no longer slaves of sin which leads to death. Rather they have been freed from its power and are now servants of God and of righteousness (6:15-23).

In Rom. 6:14, Paul has introduced the law's relationship to this freedom, haunted by the problem it posed: What is the Christian's relation to the law and what is the relation of the law to sin? Here, in Romans chapter 7, Paul would argue that the believer has not only died to sin but also to the law. As a preliminary remark, it is crucial to understand what the main argument of Paul is in the chapter. It could be argued that, basically, Paul in this chapter forcefully argues for the inability of the law to produce righteousness or to sanctify. Freedom from the law, as in the case of sin, is made possible only through Christ Jesus. The chapter could be broadly divided into two sections. The first section is comprised of verses 1-6, which are an introduction to Paul's answer with respect to the question of the believer's relation to law and sin. The section also lays the foundation for the larger section (vv. 7-25) where Paul explains the relationship between law and sin. Paul's present discussion is related to what he said in 6:14, that the Christian is "not under law but grace."[34] In the basic pattern of thought, Rom. 7:1-6 continues Rom. 6.[35] Although expressing it in a different way, Paul is dealing with the same problem in chapter 7 that occupied his attention in chapter 6—sanctification, or the believers' freedom in Christ. Paul continues to emphasize the believers' freedom but with more focus on the law. The opening verses of Romans 7 explain the statement in 6:14 that Christians are not "under law." Only living people are subject to law—and Christians have died. In sharing

Christ's death (cf. 6.2-11), they "died to the law" and may now "bear fruit for God" (7:4). This suggests, of course, that at least they did not "bear such fruit" because it was impossible do so as long as they were "under" the law; and indeed, a close connection between sin and the law was implied in 6:14. These latter implications are developed in 7:5-6. What the law arouses are "sinful passions," and these lead to death; release from the law, by way of contrast, is followed by new and effective service to God. The objections raised to Paul's position in 6:1 and 15 have now been answered: No, Christians are not to continue in sin, for a fundamental change in their condition has taken place. They have been set free from sin and are to serve God in the Spirit.

**Explanation A New Relation: Illustration from Marriage (7:1-6)**

1. Or do you not know, brethren (for I am speaking to those who know the law), that the law has jurisdiction over a person as long as he lives? 2. For the married woman is bound by law to her husband while he is living; but if her husband dies, she is released from the law concerning the husband. 3. So then if, while her husband is living, she is joined to another man, she shall be called an adulteress; but if her husband dies, she is free from the law, so that she is not an adulteress, though she is joined to another man. 4. Therefore, my brethren, you also were made to die to the law through the body of Christ, that you might be joined to another, to Him who was raised from the dead, that we might bear fruit for God. 5. For while we were in the flesh, the sinful passions, which were aroused by the law, were at work in the members of our body to bear fruit for death. 6. But now we have been released from the law, having died to that by which we were bound, so that we serve in newness of the Spirit and not in oldness of the letter.

In the same manner as he did in Rom. 6:3, Paul starts the section with the question do you not know?" He thus assumes some knowledge on the part of his readers.[36] With this question, Paul is pointing the Roman Christians backward to 6:1-14 where Paul has discussed the believer's dying to sin and its implications. Dying to sin opens up the possibility of walking in the newness of life. Now he focuses on v. 14 and sharpens his argument by reminding them of the legal principle that "death frees from former obligations" (7:1-3).

In Rom. 7:1, Using the same word, *kyrieuei*,[37] that he previously did in Rom. 6:9, 14, Paul establishes a connection between law, sin, and death—a connection which was more than casual. To appreciate the connection one only needs to look at the use of the word in chapters 6 and 7. In Rom. 6:9 it is used in the context of the death and resurrection of Christ where the inability of death to reign as lord over him is shown. However in 6:14, "For sin shall not reign over you, for you are not under the law but under grace," it is connected with sin, where it is portrayed as a reigning lord, "exercising lordship" or "reigning over." Sin could therefore be described as "lord." Curiously enough, it is here Paul links the reigning of sin with the law, a fact that suggests a relationship. This relationship is not clearly defined by Paul in this passage. Paul leaves that until Rom. 7:7-13. A significant point to be observed is the negative temporal future in 6:14, "shall not reign," which suggests a condition after salvation. Paul was talking about those who had already died to sin. However in 7:1 Paul states that the law reigns over a living person, using the present tense, which would make the verse look more like the description of a person before salvation. One could draw a conclusion that whatever experiences the two indicative statements may be pointing to, the condition of the person described is prior to conversion. The connection between freedom from sin and freedom from the law must therefore be a close one. The extent of the close relationship is not clearly defined until verse 5.

To reinforce his argument, Paul, in verse 2, employs the analogy of marriage, not only to emphasize but to heighten the spiritual motivation for sanctification. As a commonly accepted fact both among Jews and Gentiles, Paul argues, a woman is bound to her husband as long as he lives. If he should die, she is released from the obligation to her husband. Were she to do otherwise, that is, be married to another man while her husband lives, she would of course be an adulteress. But if her husband is dead, she is free from the obligation that bound her to her husband and may be married to another man. Christians, according to Paul, have died to the law because of Christ's own death. They have now been brought into a new relationship with Christ. It can hardly be denied that what

Paul says points back to the conversion experience of death to sin and resurrection to new life—an experience that brought new spiritual purpose and new moral power—all to the end that believers should bring forth fruit unto God.

In v. 4, we find one of the greatest statements of this whole book, as Paul draws a conclusion from the analogy of marriage, "Therefore, my brethren, you also were made to die to the Law through the body of Christ, that you might be joined to another, to Him who was raised from the dead, so that we might bear fruit for God." This conclusion, introduced by the inferential particle therefore, is grounded on the principle stated in v. 1 and illustrated in vv. 2-3. It is through Christ's death on the cross that the believer dies to the law. Through Christ, believers have been made to die to the law and are now married to Christ. Although individually experienced, the communal dimension of believer's experience must not be missed here. This is implied by the "divine passive" of being made to die to the law, a reference to Christ's death "for all" on the cross. We take His name. The purpose of the believers' union with Christ, expressed by the phrase "died to the law," Paul states, is that they might bring forth fruits to God. The implications are staggering. We are to submit ourselves to Him and not to run our lives by ourselves anymore. How often we think of sanctification in terms of what it means to us and brings to us. It is like a person who marries for money or inheritance. Although the believer may rejoice , and rightly so for the inestimable riches in Christ, it is clear that we have an obligation to be fruitful for Him. Of what fruit does Paul speak? Without doubt, he speaks of the fruit of the Spirit (Gal. 5:22, 23) and of a holy life. Paul's language suggests that he has ethical holiness in mind.

In Rom. 7:5, Paul defines the relationship by portraying the law as the beach-head of sin, resulting in death. The law is shown as the stimulant of sinful passions. The sphere of influence that controls life before conversion is sin, which is personified by Paul and viewed as a tyrant. Law is one of those tyrannies that functioned under sin. It has been manipulated by sin to fulfil its own purpose, other than the one for which it was intended. Sin is the real culprit and has commandeered law by bringing it into the sphere of sin and the flesh to accomplish death. Thus, to be under the law means to live in the sphere of influence under which the law operated as an agent of sin. The corollary is necessarily to be seen as true, that is, to be dead to the law means to have been transferred out of that sphere of influence in which the law has functioned negatively. If sin and the law are so related, death to one means death to the other. A disjunction is thus impossible.

In verse 6, Paul continues his thought on the believers' death to the law, by the use of a contrast—"but now"— between the believers' past and present situation. Here, Paul contrasts the believer's present situation to the pre-conversion life. It is probably used intentionally to describe further what Paul means by justification. It was to show that the doctrine of justification presupposes not only the righteousness of God,[38] but also that one needs to be put right with God. It presupposes that humanity apart from Christ, that is, outside faith, remains in bondage to the powers of the present evil age (sin and death), to sin's "host" (the flesh),[39] and to sin's agent (the law). Paul's exposition of the believer's death to the law is carried further by his affirmation that "we have been discharged from the law." Paul thus expresses the same thought as in verse 4. The phrase, "dying to that in which we were bound," explains in the language taken from v. 4, the manner of the believer's release from the law. However, Paul does not stop there. He goes further to explain the result of the believer's death to the law in the next clause. We have been made to die to the law "so that we serve in the newness of the Spirit and not in the old way of the written code." Our death to the law is inseparably connected with serving in the newness of life. It seems difficult to explain the phrase "serving in newness of life" unless it is understood experientially. As such, our death to the law is not to be defined or understood in vague terms. Rather it must be understood, as we have tried to show, as a quality of life that is required of and manifested by those who have been set free.

To clarify what has been said so far, one final question must be answered. "In what experiential sense did Paul conceive the believers' dying to the law?" The answer to this question is to be explored below. First, any presentation of Paul's statements on the law cannot be separated from the biographical aspects of Paul's life. Therefore, the interpretation of the statement "die to the law" has to be dealt with on two levels: on that of his biography, which can be reconstructed from his letters, and on that of the law statements in his epistles, especially in Romans and Galatians.[40]

In Gal. 2:19, Paul states "For through the law I died to the law." In this verse, Paul presents in a nutshell the essence of his own theology. Paul here talks about his own death to the law in a manner reminiscent of Rom. 7:1-6. Although the word "I" may be taken either in a strict personal sense or paradigmatically,[41] it seems inconceivable to see the word as completely devoid of personal overtone or lacking reference to a personal concrete experience.[42] However, one should be careful not to limit what Paul was saying to his personal experience, since what he is saying is valid for every Christian.[43] Here, to the law and for God , (cf. Rom. 6:2; 10-11) are placed over against each other to indicate to whom the believer belongs and is subject to. Paul once again reveals his thought of the law as a power that is hostile to (sinful) man, which brings him under its jurisdiction, which obstructs the way to life. To this law Paul has now died. His death with Christ (crucifixion with Christ), which he goes on to discuss in the latter part of the verse, results in death to the law and its slavish control.

Christ's death satisfied the demands of the law and nullified its lordship both over him and and over those who are bound in solidarity with him, those who, like him, have died to sin. Believers, of whom Paul was representative, have been crucified with Christ as a result of which they had become free from the bondage of the law. They are now free to live a mode of existence that is no longer dominated by law.[44] The thought here is that, as in Christ's death on the cross, the believer has died to the powers of sin, world and law, so also in the resurrection of Christ he has been set at liberty for God, in order to live for him, under his control. The demands of the law have been fully satisfied and therefore, the law has no more hold on the believer.

The positive side of dying to the law is indicated in the subordinate clause, "that I may live for God" (Gal. 2:19). The affinity of these verses with the passage in Rom. 6:3 appears at several points. For Paul, freedom means transfer from one dominion to another: from law to grace (Rom. 6:14), from sin to righteousness (Rom. 6:18), from death to life (Rom. 6:21-23), and in this place, from self to Christ. This is the very essence of the believer's faith-union relationship with God. This relationship has sometimes been understood in terms of service to others, that is, in terms of discipleship. It is certainly more than that. The phrase is reminiscent of Rom. 6:10. It should be viewed in terms of the believer's faith relationship with Christ. In speaking of the believer's past resurrection with Christ, Paul has in view as well an experience in the actual life history of the believer. Paul is talking in terms of a faith-union relationship with Christ, which, we argue, begins at conversion or baptism. Being raised with Christ is an aspect of being joined with him existentially. It may be said, then, that what holds true for resurrection is simply a reflection of the broader, more basic concept of union.

As argued above, the connection between law and sin leads us back to "we have died to sin" in Rom. 6:2. If this interpretation is correct, it means that the believer died to the law at the same time that he died to sin. The argument in this section can be summed up as follows: (1) The law has jurisdiction only over the living (7:1); as a result, the Christian who has died "through the body of Christ" is no longer bound by the law. (2) A wife is at liberty from the law that binds her to the husband upon his death; the Christian is like that wife whose husband had died. Just as she is free from "the law of the husband," so through death the Christian is freed from the law (7:2,3). The law is no longer our master, because we do not have to obey it in order to live. The motivation for sanctification is not any longer the legal requirement, but spiritual allegiance and inward affection (7:5,6). The real issue in these verses (7:1-6) is that, when death brings an end to the marriage bond, the wife is free to remarry and begin a new life. This is implied by the expression, "become to another husband," which is used twice in v. 3, and repeated in v. 4. It shows that, in addition to the point that death severs one's relationship with the law, Paul was showing in vv. 2-3 that such a death opens the possibility of entering into a new relationship. The analogy should therefore be understood in light of what Paul said in chapter 6. Freedom from the law does not leave one in a neutral, uncommitted state. It is not possible to remain "unmarried." Therefore, the suggestion that the main purpose here is not to describe the believer's situation but to drive home the "single point" that death liberates from the law[45] seems to have missed the whole argument of Paul in this passage.[46] This conclusion seems to be a deliberate neglect or downplaying of the factuality of the indicative statements. The indicative concepts are factual statements that suggest a historical reality. The Christian has entered into a new relationship with God through Christ. From the exegetical discussion above, it seems justifiable to conclude that the concept "died to the law," is best understood and becomes intelligible only within the context of the believer's existential faith-union relationship with Christ. While it is conceivable to think of the believer's dying to the law as an act accomplished by God, that is, a divine passive in which case God counts Christ's death to be ours, it is also important to understand that the believer's dying to the law is neither theoretical nor merely psychological. It was an actual death which is conceivable only in terms of participation in Christ's death, hence, union with Christ remains an underlying factor. Further, the believer's faith-union relationship with Christ is real and experiential. Hence, it can be precisely defined or at least described. It speaks of the believer's new life in Christ that begins when he is converted.

As a conclusion to this section, it needs be emphasised that the believer's freedom from the law and sin is neither to be construed as or mistaken for a freedom from the temptation to sin. Paul adamantly warns those who have been liberated from sin to be on guard (cf. 6.12-13). The believer has died to sin; however, sin is not dead. This is also part of the Christian paradox where the believer is freed into slavery. When the believer dies to sin and the Law, he/she is free. However, this is not freedom *from* God, this is freedom *to* God. Christians becomes love-slaves to God and are only free to do what pleases God.

## Character and Purpose of the Law (7:7-13)

7. What shall we say then? Is the Law sin? May it never be! On the contrary, I would not have come to know sin except through the Law; for I would not have known about coveting if the Law had not said, "You shall not covet." 8. But sin, taking opportunity through the commandment, produced in me coveting of every kind; for apart from the Law sin is dead. 9. And I was once alive apart from the Law; but when the commandment came, sin became alive, and I died; 10. and this commandment, which was to result in life, proved to result in death for me; 11. for sin, taking opportunity through the commandment, deceived me, and through it killed me. 12. So then, the Law is holy, and the commandment is holy and righteous and good. 13. Therefore did that which is good become a cause of death for me? May it never

be! Rather it was sin, in order that it might be shown to be sin by effecting my death through that which is good, that through the commandment sin might become utterly sinful.

Up to v. 6, Paul has spoken about dying to the law in the same way as he did about dying to sin. He has portrayed the law as if it were an enemy, and like something evil. But Paul would argue otherwise. God's law is good. In verses 7-25 Paul demonstrates this as he shows the effects of God's law in people's lives. What Paul has just said in the opening in 7:1-6 gives rise to the question, "Is the law sin?" If the law—or any moral standard—cannot help humans, if the only thing it does is to stir up sin, is it bad in itself? And just how does it stir up sin? Anticipating these questions, Paul proceeds to explain. His reaction to the suggestion that the law is sin is utter horror: "God forbid!" Paul goes on to show that the law of God is good, provided we understand its function to point out sin. The law is utterly impotent as a means of salvation, and it is insufficient to produce righteousness. Already Paul has said, "By the law is the knowledge of sin" (3:20); also, the law came in "that the offence might abound" (5:20). He has said that sinful passions are aroused by the law (7:5). His purpose now is to show that the law is good for its purpose but that it cannot relieve the soul suffering under the conviction of sin or be the means of effecting the righteousness that ought to characterize the life of the saved person. Let me offer an illustration here. I have had the privilege of living in three continents—Africa, Asia and North America, over an extended period of time. In the early 1970's, if I recall correctly, there were no traffic lights in Lagos, Nigeria. To ensure a smooth flow of traffic, there were only a few traffic signs, and traffic policemen were stationed at only some of the major intersections. The result? It is like the postscript of the book of Judges—"everyone did what was right in his own eyes" (Judges 21:25b). I later moved to one of the biggest cities in Asia (Manila, Philippines), where there were more traffic lights and traffic policemen. Yet people drove and deliberately flouted the laws, sometimes not afraid of being caught. I now live in the United States where everything is written in black and white. There are more detailed traffic regulations, speed limits and more traffic enforcers. Yet the story appears to be the same. I have seen people beating traffic lights, and there also are ways of getting around the law—technological gadgets and devices that make law breaking easier. What do we learn from this? First we learn that humans are the same regardless of their geographical and social locations. Second, and more importantly for our purpose, we see that although laws are good, obedience to laws requires a change of heart. In theological terms, it begins with regeneration. Obedience and righteousness, although they can be legislated, cannot be enforced.

One may ask, are the traffic lights and regulations bad? Of course not, anyone would say. They are meant for our well-being and protection. Besides, they let us know what the acceptable standards are. This is the argument that Paul is about to pursue, starting from verse 7. In this verse Paul shows that, although the law is "by no means" sin, the fact remains that it is closely connected with sin; for apart from the law "I" would have had no personal experience ("knowledge") of sin. In other words, consciousness of sin is only possible where law exists to be transgressed. This is in agreement with what Paul has said earlier in 5:13 that without law, there is no accounting for sin. No guilt is entailed and sin is not effective on people. Paul uses the illustration of the tenth commandment: "I had not known lust, except the law had said, 'Thou shalt not covet'." The commandment against coveting arouses the desire to covet. How true to life this is! When something is prohibited, we want it all the more. This shows something not only of the natural perversity of humankind but also of the necessity of salvation and grace. Ethical instructions and the law would not suffice.

Paul says further that sin receives incentive from the commandment to work "all manner of concupiscence" or every kind of evil desire. When the law commands, "Thou shalt not," it seems to stir up the strongest sort of desire for violation and wrongdoing. Apart from the law, sin is dead, or seems to be in a dormant state. But let the law point it out, and then sin comes to life and springs into action. In a further testimony out of experience, Paul refers to his former sense of false security. "I was alive without the law once." The law showed Paul that many of his thoughts and deeds were wrong (vv. 7, 9). It showed him that he was in fact sinful and spiritually dead—alienated from God. What is the role of the law in all of these? One could perhaps liken the law to a plumb-line which shows the bricklayer that a wall that seemed to be quite straight is actually crooked.

The law, like light, reveals the hidden things of darkness and drags them out into the open day. As the sun's rays shining in a window expose hitherto unseen dust particles in the air, so the law reveals the character of sin. Paul's own testimony about coveting is an example. Something happened to make the commandments of God real, and then sin revived. It became alive and made Paul conscious of his death in sin. Without the law, one is in a state of spiritual stupor. Christians too can learn a truth here. We can get to the place where sin doesn't seem so sinful anymore. That is why we must be thoughtful and diligent readers of God's word. The word of God will either keep us from sin or sin will keep us from the word. Individuals may live happily for many years until they begin to realise that things in their lives that they thought were right are indeed wrong. The realisation of sinfulness does not come until one realises God's standard of righteousness—how God wants one to live.

Paul states that the commandment, therefore, which was holy and good and meant for life, became the means of death. Actually, it was not the law of God, but sin, Paul says, "taking occasion by the commandment, deceived me, and by it slew me." The law was only the tool or instrument; sin did its deceptive and deadly work. What Paul says is an exact description of the power of sin. It deceives and slays. It never gives up in its effort to thwart and defeat Christian sanctification. But God's grace is sufficient.

The central truth in this paragraph is emphasized again in verses 12-13. Paul pays the highest commendation to the law. The commandment is holy and just and good. The purpose of the law is to point out sin, to awaken the conscience, to make humans aware of moral duty and spiritual need. It makes sin appear as sin. It shows that sin is exceedingly sinful. There is nothing wrong with the law. The wrong is in the heart, in the addiction to sin. Let us keep clearly in mind the central purpose in what Paul says. He does not disparage the moral law as a moral guide. He does not say that the Christian is not under obligation to obey the law. He defends the law for its true function; but he declares again and again that the righteousness of God can never be the product of the law. What has been said so far can be summarised as follows: First, Paul argues that the law is holy, and the commandment is holy and just and good. Nevertheless, it is still not true that justification or sanctification comes by the law. The law is powerless to make a person do good. It can only convict a person of sin in his/her life. In fact the law rouses up sin, and makes it more active (vs. 7). The law reveals sin for what it really is. And that is why the law was given. Now we see clearly the relationship between this statement about the purpose of the law and the first section of the chapter which states that as Christians we are free from the law. If the law cannot justify but only condemn, it is necessary for us to get free from its demands. This has been made possible through Christ. But some of the Jews, no doubt, will take issue with Paul over this unusual interpretation of the law. And they will try to prove to him that he is wrong by saying, "Look at the average Jew under the law. Would you say that it is serving to convict him of sin? No, the average Jew actually believes that he is being justified by the law, not condemned by it. So Paul, you are wrong; the purpose of the law is not what you say it is! Far from it." Consequently, the latter part of the chapter (vv. 14-25) is an illustration on the part of Paul of how the law functions in humans exactly in accordance with the purpose he has just stated. The law reveals to a person the extent of the sin which operates in humans. The cardinal lesson to be learned from this section is that the law can tell us what to do. However it cannot provide or impart the power needed to carry out its requirements. It does no more than show us the necessity to conform to a standard. It can enlighten the conscience, but it fails to produce holiness of life.

**Operation of the Law (7:14-25)**

14. For we know that the law is spiritual; but I am of flesh, sold into bondage to sin. 15. For that which I am doing, I do not understand; for I am not practicing what I would like to do, but I am doing the very thing I hate. 16. But if I do the very thing I do not wish to do, I agree with the law, confessing that it is good. 17. So now, no longer am I the one doing it, but sin which indwells me. 18. For I know that nothing good dwells in me, that is, in my flesh; for the wishing is present in me, but the doing of the good is not. 19. For the good that I wish, I do not do; but I practice the very evil that I do not wish. 20. But if I am doing the very thing I do not wish, I am no longer the one doing it, but sin which dwells in me. 21. I find then the principle that evil is present in me, the one who wishes to do good. 22. For I joyfully concur with the law

of God in the inner man, 23. but I see a different law in the members of my body, waging war against the law of my mind, and making me a prisoner of the law of sin which is in my members. 24. Wretched man that I am! Who will set me free from the body of this death? 25. Thanks be to God through Jesus Christ our Lord! So then, on the one hand I myself with my mind am serving the law of God, but on the other, with my flesh the law of sin.

As mentioned earlier at the beginning of this chapter, this section of the Book of Romans has probably been debated more than any other part. One could say that, without doubt, it has been subject to misunderstanding, misinterpretation and misappropriation. What are the reasons for this problem? First, is the change in tense from the past (aorist) to the present which has made some to conclude that Paul must have been speaking of his state at the time of writing—a reference to Paul's post-conversion experience of Paul—a view advocated by the Reformers, although understood somewhat differently. Other scholars have noted grammatical possibilities that do not require the use of the present tense to be a depiction of Paul's on-going experience when he was writing. As such, it is argued, the present tense is only a dramatic and vivid presentation of what Paul experienced, albeit retrospectively. Thus, Paul must be understood as speaking here of those under the law and without Christ. With greater appreciation for Paul's use of rhetorical conventions, Stowers, for example, has argued that Paul's form of argument here conforms with what is known as speech-in-character, the standard Greco-Latin rhetorical device of *prosopopoiia* where the author is describing someone else's experience.[47] He contends that Paul's speech in Rom. 7:7-25 about the conflict between the law of the mind and the law of the flesh is not actually a description of his own struggles, but rather, Paul is speaking in the character of a gentile who has gone from paganism to Judaism to Christianity.

The second problem with the passage is Paul's switch from the first person plural in vv. 7-13 to the singular form in vv. 14-25, which, to some, reinforces the suggestion that the passage is autobiographical. The third problem, although not clearly stated in textbooks, is the fact that the experience described in the passage resonates with that of many believers. For such people, this passage provides the best illustration of the constant tension in the Christian life. Believers, it is argued, continue to experience a spiritual bifurcation. What exactly is Paul saying in these verses?

In verse 14, Paul continues his argument on the holy character of the law and its powerlessness. That this section is connected with the preceding is beyond question. A casual reading may suggest that the focus in this section is not on the law as such but on the existential predicament of humanity which is expressed vividly and picturesquely. However, a more careful reading suggests that these two sections (vv. 7-13; 14-25) are two different perspectives on the same problem, namely, the inability of the law to sanctify. Paul continues to show that the law can only stimulate sin and condemn humans, because it is powerless in the face of sin. The passage is not a digression but a continued clarification of what Paul has said so far. He says, "For we know that the Law is spiritual; but I am of flesh, sold into bondage to sin." Paul declares again that the fault is not with the law, that is, the law of God. This law is spiritual; it is the gift of God. The fault is with the law of sin, which is a part of the depravity of human nature. Paul declares, "I am carnal, sold under sin." The word translated "carnal" means made of flesh—wholly given up to the flesh, rooted in the flesh, as it were. In this context, being in the flesh is to be understood in terms of human-ness. Paul declares that he is a creature of the flesh, as all people are. This does not mean that the flesh is inherently evil, but it does mean that it is "sold under sin," in captivity to sin. Sin has obtained access into it, has taken up its residence there and from that base of operations has brought the whole personality into slavery. In its presumption to live righteously before the law on the basis of its own capacities, flesh becomes subjugated to the greater power of sin and consequently to the greater power of death. It is therefore inappropriate to understand flesh as a type of sin nature that makes believers remain as *simul justus et peccator* (justified and sinful simultaneously), awaiting complete victory only when the body dies. The major problem, we have noted earlier is the latter part of this verse. Who does Paul have in mind by "I" that is sold under sin, and described in the rest of the section?

First, one must begin by considering Paul's language of being sold in v.14. The word Paul uses here is used for the selling of slaves (cf. Mt.18:25).

The imagery of slavery harks back to Rom. 6:15-23 where the believer is shown as a person that is liberated from slavery to sin but continues to be a slave of righteousness. Could Paul have been liberated in chapter 6 and become enslaved to sin in chapter 7 again? The answer must be a resounding "No." Futhermore, it is to be noted that Paul uses the perfect tense *pepramenos*, which literally means "having been sold." In this regard, one should remember that the perfect tense indicates an action that took place but continues to have an effect. That is not a picture of a truly liberated person.

Second, beginning from verse 15, Paul describes a picture of helplessness, or may we say hopelessness, for the "I" in the previous verse. The very fact that the person described here continues in a real tension between what he knows to be right and what he actually achieves attests to Paul's declaration that the law (that is, the law of God) is good. Such a total spiritual wretchedness described here and in the following verses is irreconcilable with the saving grace of God. It seems best to see the graphic picture that Paul painted here as that of humanity outside Christ in general and his retrospective view of his own life lived under the law prior to coming to Christ—a life that is now seen through the lenses of his new life and relationship with Christ. Once again, we must remember that the main message of 6:1-7:6 that freedom from tyrannical domination of sin and the law are now possible in Christ. Hence, a few questions are *apropos* at this juncture.

How could Paul, describing a situation of tension in his Christian experience, say that he was sold under sin?—Where then is the freedom from sin which he insists on in the previous chapter? Is not the expression, "I see in my members another law. . . making me captive to the law of sin which dwells in my members" entirely opposite to his teaching elsewhere, if it refers to his Christian experience? Can he, as a Christian, say that he is made captive to the law of sin? He has already in this very chapter said, "We are discharged from the law, dead to that which held us captive" (v. 6). If we say that Paul is referring to an inner struggle in his Christian life, then we must admit that he in the same chapter has made contrary statements. That, however, is not the case. Paul here is simply illustrating what he was referring to in the earlier section and describing his condition and feelings while under the law.

Third, as was shown in discussion of Rom. 6, Paul vigorously maintained that believers are no longer in bondage to sin. Also, in 7:6 he said we have been discharged from the law. How could he turn around in 7:14-25 and say that he is now a slave of sin? If so, Paul contradicts himself by saying that he was both sold under sin and freed from sin at the same time. The language is not only far too strong to describe an ongoing Christian experience, but totally inconsistent with the clear teaching of Paul elsewhere. He boldly declares that he has been crucified with Christ and that Christ lives in him. At the same time he says that those who belong to Christ have crucified the flesh with its sinful desires (Gal 2:20; 5:24). Paul has told the Roman Christians in the previous section of the possibility of victory over sin as he proclaims, "For sin will have no dominion over you, since you are not under law, but under grace" etc.). By the example of his own life and proclamation Paul demonstrates both the possibility and the power of grace. Rom. 8 provides the picture of such life.

Fourth, to the objection that the referent of the "I" is a regenerate person because of the "delight in the law of God" (v. 22), one may question whether a delight in the law of God is necessarily the result of being in a dynamic, ongoing covenant relationship with God. The Pharisees provide an example in this regard. They desired a relationship with God, but on their own terms; the works of the law. Pharisaism took seriously the basically cultic Torah and extended it to the everyday life of the Jews so there were strict regulations with regard to purity or holiness. The Pharisees sought to live in the world without being contaminated by it. Pharisees took seriously the need for Israel as a whole to seek holiness and saw how important it was to make the law relevant for the contemporary situation. But they did not succeed. Their failure was not due to lack of trying. The law was grossly inadequate to effect the holiness that is required by God. The deep longings for holiness, for freedom from sin, should not surprise us in the life of Paul under the law, because there were people who had deep longings for holiness even under the law. This must be an experience Paul had prior to his conversion, which he was now relating from the vantage point of faith. This is the experience of somebody now looking back saying, "this is the way I lived. This was my life under the law." Is it not a matter of fact that there are in the twenty-first century many people who delight in the word and who read and study God's word more than those who claim to be the people of God?

David delighted in the law as the Old Testament scriptures attest. The Psalms are replete with distinct statements and commands of David concerning his delight in the law of God. But David knew that relationship with God was not by the way of the law. Paul has already alluded to David's experience in Rom. 4, as we saw in the preceding chapter. Hence, to suggest that an unregenerate person could not delight in God's law is surely a false conclusion. Delighting in the law of God must not be equated with entering into a covenant relationship with God. The deep longings for holiness, for freedom from sin should not surprise us in the life of Paul under the law, because there were people who had deep longings for holiness even under the law. This must be an experience Paul had prior to his conversion which he was now relating from the vantage point of faith. This is the experience of somebody now looking back saying, "this is the way I lived. This was my life under the law."

In v. 25, instead of providing a specific answer to the question that he raised in the previous verse, but having given a long description of humanity apart from Christ, represented by himself, Paul comes out with the answer to his and humanity's great problem as he exclaims " Thanks be to God through Jesus Christ out Lord." This, then, is the right conclusion to the chapter. It is the expression of jubilation, which is out of place, but only because Paul could contain himself no longer. It is a preview of what he is going to enlarge upon in chapter eight. To recapitulate then, we find that the primary teaching of this seventh chapter is that in Christ we are free from the law. The main purpose of the law is to convict humans of their sinful condition. Paul shows how that came to pass in his own life. He intimates what the full solution to the problem of sin is in his exultant, "Thanks be to God, through our Lord Jesus Christ." The Christian life ought to be an experience of growing victory over sin, but let no one expect that he will not have to fight the tempter before the victory is won.

What Paul has done in chapter 7 is to strip away every aspect of the privileges the Jews may claim to have—the Torah law of Rom. 7:1 gradually shifting to the "law of the Spirit" (Rom. 8:2). Jews and Gentiles stand together as ones who have "no condemnation for those who are in Christ Jesus" (Rom. 8:1). Romans 7:14-25 is atypical of Paul's portrayal of the life of faith and, therefore, should never be considered as the centerpiece of Paul's view of the Christian life. One thing is clear: the meaning of the passage cannot be decided solely by grammar. The passage is to be understood as the description of an unregenerate person viewed from the vantage point of faith. There is continuity of theme across the supposed division between 7:7-13 and 7:13-25. In other words, 7:7-25 should be read as a whole. The experience Paul describes in 7:7-13 is exactly the same experience he describes in 7:14-25. It is an experience of failure, despite one's best efforts. The only change, apart from tense, is perhaps a move from a specific personal example to the general condition of those seeking to serve by the written code. It is therefore unfortunate that many people, through the past centuries and until the present, have attempted to produce doctrines based upon their own experiences. For many years, the lament of the 'wretched man' in Rom. 7:14-25 has comforted many people as they yield to various temptations to sin. However, the life of constant defeat shown in this passage is completely contrary to the believer's new life as portrayed in chapters six through eight. Specifically Rom. 6:1-7:6 shows that believers are free from sin and the law through their participation in the death and resurrection of Jesus Christ. Within the immediate context and its focus on the law, the passage of 7:14-25 emphasizes the plight of searching for sanctification without faith and highlights the frustration of seeking freedom by the law.

In conclusion, the idea that the Christian is powerless and does the very thing he or she hates is to be seen as not only repugnant, and therefore to be rejected, but also is contrary to Christ's and the New Testament writers' call for repentance, discipleship and holy living. Indeed no Christian, such as is portrayed in chapter 6, would cry, "wretched man that I am!" Romans 7 should not be understood either as a description or prescriptive norm of the Christian life. If that is the kind of Christian life we have, then it is non-Pauline and substandard. Verses 14-25 are more than a mere moral frustration. Instead, what we have is a moral failure, which does not sound or look like a life transformed by grace and led by the Spirit as we find in chapters 6-8.

Based upon Paul's extensive use of literary devices in his rhetorical writings and the bridge of solidarity that he was extending to the Jews, it appears that Paul used the present tense "I" in an effort to strengthen his solidarity with the Jews and for its dramatic effect. Paul is emphasizing the struggle with sin and with being under the law before gaining victory 'in Christ'. Unfortunately, many people do not want to hear that they can live without sin; however, it is inaccurate to use the passage of 7:14-25 to validate an unrighteous lifestyle. 'Thanks be to God through Jesus Christ our Lord!' (7:25) that Christians are not consigned to wallow in sin, but are instead challenged and encouraged through Paul's writing to live within their hopeful Christian existence because they are no longer condemned to a life of struggling with sin.

# Chapter 4

## But By My Spirit—Romans 8:1-39

It happened sometime in 1979. After several failed attempts to help, I decided to report a young man who was a drunkard and yet professed to be an active member of a Pentecostal Church to his pastor for counselling and help. Then came the strangest answer that I could ever imagine. The pastor asked the young man, "Have you been baptised or filled with the Holy Spirit?" The young man answered with an emphatic "No". The pastor told me that was the problem. I was much disappointed and never ceased to wonder what the pastor meant by being spirit filled or what the baptism of the Holy Spirit had to do with someone who, by evangelical standard, needed to hear the message of repentance. The short story I have just related underscores the importance of a proper understanding and articulation of what Spirit-filled living is and how it relates to sanctification.

Without doubt, we live in the age of the Holy Spirit. Many would agree that we are witnessing the fulfilment of Joel's prophecy beyond the initial outpouring of the Holy Spirit on the day of Pentecost. Evidence and proofs of the activity of the Holy Spirit abound everywhere. Yet, it appears that a crucial issue is often overlooked, misunderstood and, consequently, insufficiently addressed. That issue is the relationship of the Holy Spirit to Pauline ethics, particularly sanctification or holiness. In this regard, several important questions may be raised. What is the role of the Holy Spirit both in the process and maintenance of sanctification? Is there any relationship between Spirit-baptism and sanctification? If there is, what is the nature of this relationship? Are both one and the same experience, as has sometimes been suggested by some or are both mutually exclusive?

For example, the issue that has clearly separated many Wesleyans from Pentecostals is the question of the relationship between the experiences of sanctification and the baptism with the Holy Spirit. Generally, Wesleyans have equated sanctification to be the same as Spirit-baptism, regarding the former as the evidence of the latter.[48] On the other hand, many Pentecostals have tended to neglect sanctification as a necessary experience, distinct from, and prior to spirit-baptism. Instead, the emphasis lies on speaking in tongues as well as power for service. What then is Spirit-filled living? The following is an attempt to answer this important question by examining Rom. 8, a crucial passage where Paul constantly mentions the role of the Holy Spirit in connection with sanctification.

In order to fully appreciate and understand the truth about sanctification and the role of the Holy Spirit in its outworking, one must set the interpretation of the chapter in its context. As stated earlier in this book, the chapter is part of a larger section beginning with the sixth chapter. In the earlier chapters of Romans Paul has dealt with universal sinfulness, the need for salvation, and God's provision through Christ. Beginning with chapter 6, Paul begins to show the obligation of the Christian to live a new kind of life.[49] Christians must yield themselves as slaves to God and righteousness. In chapter 7, we have seen that such life is not possible through human efforts, particularly by relying on the law. Looking through chapter 7, one could not but notice the sparse reference to the saving and sanctifying activity of Christ or the Spirit. This is especially true in vv. 7-25, particularly in the controversial section of vv. 14-25. The mention of Christ and the Spirit pale in comparison with what one finds in chapters 6 and 8. Thus, coming after such an important passage where Paul describes the struggle of the person who seeks to fulfil the demands of Christ by obedience to the law rather than faith, one cannot but appreciate the significance of the role of the Holy Spirit in Chapter 8.

Full weight must be given to chapter 8. In many ways, it caps the whole argument on sanctification in the three chapters. [50] The chapter gathers up the central intent of the two previous chapters and takes the key points further.[51] It does so by showing the connection between the newness of life that characterises the one that has died to sin with the Spirit and, at the same time, by connecting the fulfillment of the Law with the Spirit. As Paul would argue in this chapter, Christ's salvific work does not nullify the call of God to live a holy life—quite the contrary: because of the Spirit, God brings to fulfillment in the community of faith the "just requirements of the Law" (8:1-5). The unquestionable emphasis in this chapter, then, is upon the life that is lived by the power of the Holy Spirit.[52] It is significant to note that prior to this point in the letter there are only four references (Rom. 1:4; 2:29; 5:5; 7:6) to the Holy Spirit, compared to twenty-one in this chapter (Rom. 8:2, 4, 5 (2), 6, 9 (3), 10, 11(2), 13, 14, 15 (2), 16 (2), 23, 26 (2), 27), more than in any other chapter in the whole Bible.

Furthermore, in contrast to Rom. 7, Paul shows in this chapter that the solution to the human problem of sin is not through the law, that is through legalistic regulations, but is a life lived under the discipline, guidance and direction of the Holy Spirit.[53] Life in the Spirit is that which is characterised as life in which God's will is fulfilled, a life that even now bears the promise of resurrection and eternal life, a life that is lived in hope, and a life that experiences the victory of God in the midst of the adverse circumstances of life. It is therefore clear that Rom. 8 describes the ministry of the Holy Spirit in relationship to the believer. A cursory reading of these verses reveals Paul's concern about the relationship of the Holy Spirit to his ethics. For Paul, the Christian life is not to be lived by one's own efforts and strength. Rather, Paul is about to show that an adequate provision for Christian living is to be seen in the Person, presence and power of the Holy Spirit. As Fee succinctly states,

> This section (Rom. 8:1-39) climaxes the soteriological dimension of the argument that began in 1:18 and one can scarcely miss the crucial role played by the Holy Spirit. Even though its is never said quite in this way, the Spirit is the life-giving linchpin to everything that has been argued up to this point . . . nonetheless the Spirit is the experiential key to the whole: God in love is creating a people for his name, apart from the Law . . . . All of this is actualized in the church (and in the believer as well, of course) by the Spirit whom God has given.[54]

Rom. 8:1-4
1 There is therefore now no condemnation for those who are in Christ Jesus. 2 For the law of the Spirit of life in Christ Jesus has set you free from the law of sin and of death. 3 For what the Law could not do, weak as it was through the flesh, God did: sending

His own Son in the likeness of sinful flesh and as an offering for
sin, He condemned sin in the flesh, 4 in order that the requirement
of the Law might be fulfilled in us, who do not walk according to
the flesh, but according to the Spirit).

Most scholars and commentators would agree that these verses begin
Paul's description of what may be termed life in the Spirit—the sanctified
life. The verses link directly with Rom. 7:6.[55] Verses 1-4 are chiefly a
summary of what the Christian has become, as a result of having died to
the law (Rom. 7:6).[56] Paul starts his arguments in the chapter with the
inferential particle " therefore" to show that the discussion that follows is
a consequence of his preceding arguments. The opening words of the
chapter echo the themes of 5:1: those who have been "justified through
faith" are now "those in Christ Jesus." The benefit of "peace with God,"(cf.
Rom. 5:1) is now expressed by Paul as freedom from condemnation.
Condemnation, as Paul would stress, is completely out of the question, as
suggested by the emphatic use of the word *ouden* (none). It is significant
to note that Paul uses the same Greek noun for condemnation (*katakrima*)
in Rom. 8:1 that he uses in Rom. 5:16 and 18. Moreover, it is also
important to note that those who are free from condemnation are those
who are "in Christ Jesus."

In verse 1, Paul brings back his readers to the "now" and to his
description of the benefits of justification. It is important to note that
Paul uses the word "now" many times in his letter to the Romans (cf.
3:21, 24; 5:9; 6:19; 21). In such passages he refers to blessings that
Christians already experience. As Adam Clarke rightly notes, "the *now*
therefore, in the text must refer more to the happy transition from darkness
to light, from condemnation to pardon, which the believer now enjoys."[57]
The word *now* is temporal and distinguishes the Christian from the pre-
Christian period of life.[58]

In vv. 2-3 Paul continues his argumentation by describing the present
reality of believers. Verse 2 provides the basic truth with regards to
deliverance from sin. Christians have been "set free" from the law of sin
and death. The breakthrough or liberation is grounded upon Christ's
redemptive act—Christ has removed the believer's guilt by means of His
sacrificial death on Calvary. One may ask, "how deep and far reaching is

the freedom that Paul speaks about here?" Let's answer the question with a story: A man who had been a hard drinker was saved, and at once he dropped the liquor habit. One day he was going down the street past a tavern he formerly patronised regularly. Seeing him go by, the owner called out, "What's wrong, Charlie? Why do you keep going past instead of coming in?" Charlie paused a brief moment; then he finally replied, "It's not just me who goes past now. We go past—the Lord and I." Where sin had once abounded, grace now much more abounds (Rom. 5:20).

Only the saving acts of God in Jesus Christ, consummated through the Spirit, can free human beings from their hopeless situation (Rom. 8:2-3). Humanity, outside the saving and sanctifying grace of God and the power of the Spirit, does not possess the strength for victory. But with Christ and the Holy Spirit, victory over sin is possible. As Paul starts to lay out the contrast between living according to the flesh and living according to the Spirit, he boldly affirms that the pivot between these two ways of existing is redemption through Christ Jesus. Although Paul in the first two verses returns to the sacrificial death of Christ on the cross, he quickly shifts his focus toward a new image and dimension of the Christian experience—life in the Spirit. Paul argues that "Christ condemned sin in the flesh in order that the requirement of the Law might be fulfilled in us, who do not walk according to the flesh, but according to the Spirit."

It appears from the onset that Paul is addressing a two-fold problem with relation to sin. The first is that of assurance, and the second that of day-to-day, Spirit-filled, holy living. With regard to the first, Paul unequivocally maintains that for all who are in Christ by faith, there is no condemnation for sin, but rather the condemnation of sin in the flesh. The Christian need not be overcome by guilt or by fear, due to his or her sins. The cross of Jesus Christ is the solution from sin and its condemnation for all who are justified by faith. The death that Christ died was for all the sins of the one who receives His work by faith. Paul's arguments in 3:1-4:25 have now come full circle: The forgiveness of sins Paul describes in that section of the book applies to all the sins of the one who trusts in Christ. There is no condemnation! But there is more. While, on the one hand, Christ's death at Calvary has delivered believers from condemnation of sin, on the other hand, it also dealt a severe blow to sin, delivering it to condemnation. In Christ, God condemned sin, and that in the flesh. The flesh, though amoral, was sin's beachhead which sin used to lay hold of us and to bring us under condemnation. When God sent His Son, Jesus Christ, He came in the likeness of sinful flesh. To sum these verses up, it is evident that Paul, here, simply declares the fact of the believer's deliverance and accepts by faith that no condemnation and no bondage remains for those who have died and risen with Christ. The victory of the believer is sure and certain, for it is made possible by the Spirit. What could never be accomplished in the power of the flesh—fulfilling the righteous demand of the law, which is holiness and righteousness, is now possible through the power of the Spirit. Walking by the Spirit, Christians share the result of Christ's victory and are able to do the good things the law really wanted.

What is the import of Rom. 8:1-4? Undoubtedly, Paul's teaching in Romans 8:1-4 is central to the Christian life. There are cogent and compelling reasons to say that Paul must have had in mind the actual obedience of believers. First, the use of the passive "has been fulfilled" coupled with the prepositional phrase "in us," points in the direction that the obedience described in Rom. 8:4 is the work of God. Second, it is also hard to explain how the participle "the ones who are walking," which means to conduct one's life could refer to anything less than an actual experience of the believers. Furthermore, it is unlikely that Paul's radical antithesis of flesh and spirit is merely to be perceived or applied individualistically but also communally. The passage, although it could describe individual or group behaviours, does more than that. It is Paul's prophetic call to the Roman Christians both to a decisive commitment and to be witnesses in the society in which they lived. Kaylor sums it up well:

> The Spirit produces transformed living in which God's will comes to fulfillment in those who walk no longer according to the flesh but according to the Spirit. . . . The Spirt effects a life through renewed relationships more than a life of piety expressed in religious activity. The new life created and given by the Spirit is to be expressed in concrete living. It is not a prize possession to be placed in a case and admired, nor an insurance policy to be kept in a safe deposit-box. Rather, the new life involves anew set of relationships in which self and community are freed for life of faith expressing itself in love.[59]

Verses 5-11

For those who live according to the flesh mind the things of the flesh, but those who live according to the Spirit, the things of the Spirit. For the mind-set of the flesh is death, but the mind-set of the Spirit is life and peace; 7 because the mind set on the flesh is hostile toward God; for it does not subject itself to the law of God, for it is not even able to do so; 8 and those who are in the flesh cannot please God. 9 However, you are not in the flesh but in the Spirit, if indeed the Spirit of God dwells in you. But if anyone does not have the Spirit of Christ, he does not belong to Him. 10 And if Christ is in you, though the body is dead because of sin, yet the spirit is alive because of righteousness. 11 But if the Spirit of Him who raised Jesus from the dead dwells in you, He who raised Christ Jesus from the dead will also give life to your mortal bodies through His Spirit who indwells you.

Having stated unequivocally that those who are in Christ Jesus are now free from condemnation, Paul continues to elucidate the implications of the freedom in verse 5-11. By means of contrast, Paul draws a portrait of the one who walks or lives according to the Spirit. The section is connected with the preceding with the use of the word "for" in verse 5, although it may refer to verses 5-11 as a whole, thus providing an explanation to the reference in verse 4.

In verses 5-8 Paul clearly showed the difference between those who belong to Christ and those who do not, using the words "Spirit" and "flesh" to describe these two conditions. Flesh and spirit are not two components that produce schizophrenia in human beings so long as mortal life endures. In other words, what Paul was here saying is that you can tell what people are really like by their mind-set. Persons who belong to God direct their thoughts to the things of God and behave as new persons but those who those who think and behave as if there were no God, do so because they are "according to the flesh." "According to the flesh" in verse 5 would therefore mean the same as it does in verse 4. In these verses, one sees a stark contrast between "flesh" and "spirit." A broad treatment of Paul's use of "flesh" and "spirit" is not only unnecessary but also is impossible here. Yet it could not be denied that a proper understanding of both is crucial to the understanding of this chapter. The significant point to note is that Paul uses both terms with considerable flexibility. That being so, more often than not the meaning can be best dictated or decided by the context. The multifarious usage of these words is partly due to the variety of meanings that can be given them as standard dictionaries would show. Nevertheless certain assertions could be made on the usage of both in this passage. First, it is clear from Rom. 8:5-8 that "flesh" and "spirit" are two mutually exclusive powers that surround people and take them into service - be it death-bringing or life-giving service. Those who live by the standard of the flesh live by its dictates—they think constantly about fleshly satisfaction; but those who live by the standard of the Spirit live by his dictates and constantly have their minds set on things that please him.[60] This is the import of v. 5: "For those who live according to the flesh mind the things of the flesh, but those who live according to the Spirit, the things of the Spirit." Paul is not making a contrast of two "parts" which make up human beings, one part essentially good and the other part either problematic or essentially evil. Neither does Paul, in his use of the word "flesh" in this passage, imply "flesh" as the physical condition of being in a body of flesh and bones. Instead Paul means a particular moral and spiritual condition, as would be implied by his assertion in verse 8 that those that are in the flesh cannot please God. It should be noted that Paul is speaking in this passage about the Holy Spirit rather than the human spirit.[61] Howard's observation is straight to the point: "As plain language can state it, Paul says these two ways of living are *opposite alternatives*. They are totally irreconcilable to each other. A person can do either—*but certainly not both at the same time.*"[62]

Instead, Paul is talking about two spheres of existence—two ways of life. Paul has an optimistic view of grace that admits of triumph (not triumphalism) over sin. The consequences of walking either according to the dictates of the flesh or the Spirit are spelled out in v. 6. As John Wesley describes it, the mind set on the flesh has its "affections fixed on such things as gratify corrupt nature: namely on things visible and temporal; on things on the earth, on pleasure (of sense or imagination), praise or riches."[63] Perhaps Esau's example may be of benefit here. He was concerned only with himself; with the present time; with physical needs and interests.

He had the mind of the flesh. However, standing in contrast to the mind of the flesh is the mind of the Sprit. As Greathouse correctly observes, "If the 'mind of the flesh' is earthbound, 'the mind of the Spirit' is set on 'those things which are above, where Christ sits on the right hand of God' (Col. 3:1)."[64]

Why does Paul paint such a gloomy picture of walking in the flesh? Or, why is it futile and inexcusable? Paul proffers three reasons. First, Paul makes it clear that the flesh is hostile toward God (v. 7a). "Flesh" is not simply rebellious or being slightly uncooperative; it is downright hostility. "Neither mediation nor a natural transition between the two spheres is possible; two ontologically understood realms of power stand starkly against each other." Second, the flesh is incapable of being subject to the law of God (v. 7b). It can only produce death. A life according to the flesh means a life without access to God, a life that is captive to what is earthly and perishable.[65] Believers are obligated to walk according to the Spirit, and not according to the flesh. It is not a matter of choice. For Paul, the flesh and the Spirit share nothing in common. There is no middle ground between walking in the Spirit and walking in the flesh. Paul's exhortation does not admit of a middle ground. Third, those who follow the dictates of the flesh cannot please God (v. 8). If Romans emphasises anything, it is that salvation creates a new humanity and make a noticeable change in a person. And here the change stressed is the change in mindset—the way of thinking.

In contrast to those whose minds are set on the things of the flesh, Paul says that the Roman Christians are able to please God—they are not in hostility against God. Instead, they are in the Spirit, because God's Spirit dwells in them (Rom. 8:9-11). Life in the Spirit, Paul argues, is possible only because "the Spirit resides in you, that is, the believers." Here, it is important to note the import of the verb *oikei*, a word that means "to take up residence." From the tenor of these verses, life in the Spirit is to be understood as being more than occasionally thinking spiritual thoughts; it is even more than a supernatural influence that affects our behaviour. Rather, it is the presence (and accompanying power) of the Spirit within the believers that make living in the Spirit possible. It is the abiding presence of the Spirit which motivates the believer to develop a mind-set that is oriented toward spiritual desires. It is interesting to note that, in his argument, Paul does not negate the natural desires; instead he urges believers to bring them under the control of the Spirit.

A crucial thing that this passage suggests is the corporate dimension of believers' existence and holiness. Collectively, the Roman Christians are inhabited by the Spirit. It is thus right to suggest that the community, of which the individual is a constituent member, is in view here.[66] Paul would not have been afraid to say that the Spirit of God was taking up residence in the Roman congregation. Thus, as a congregation, it was possible for them to please God. The relationship between the one and the many is well shown in the phrase, "But if anyone does not have the Spirit of Christ, he does not belong to Him."

It is possible to draw two important inferences. First, it is possible to suggest that it is the activity of the Spirit (at justification) that effects admission into the Body of Christ. Second, following from the previous observation is the significant role of the church in maintaining or sustaining the holiness of the entire Body. The church is both the sphere of forming and maintaining holiness. Spirit-filled living is not to be the specialty or trademark of a few individuals within the congregation. It is the business of the entire body to live holy lives. Spirit-filled living or Christian holiness must never be understood as attribute of an autonomous subject; rather it is to find its limitation in the well-being of another person.

Verses 12-17
12 So then, brothers and sisters, we are not debtors to the flesh to fulfil its obligations 13 for if you are living according to the flesh, you must die; but if by the Spirit you are putting to death the deeds of the body, you will live. 14 For as many as are led by the Spirit of God, these are sons of God. 15 For ye received not the spirit of bondage again unto fear; but ye received the spirit of adoption, whereby we cry, Abba, Father. 16 The Spirit Himself bears witness with our spirit that we are children of God, 17 and if children, then heirs; heirs of God, and joint-heirs with Christ; if so be that we suffer with [him], that we may be also glorified with [him].

In Romans 8:12-17, Paul's argument is a "very closely reasoned one."[67] In verse 11 Paul states that the Spirit of God is "living in you." What follows in verse 12 is the obligation that the indwelling of the Spirit entails. In the next few verses Paul makes clear the demands on the person in whom the Spirit dwells. As a whole, verses 12-17 indicate that obedience is the hallmark of discipleship. Having spelled out the distinctive features of new life in the Spirit, he once again calls the believers to become what they are in Christ by actively participating in the work of salvation. He previously urged them to "count themselves to have died to sin" and to "offer their members to righteousness" (6:11, 13). Believers are no longer under obligation to live according to the flesh. The obligation that lies on each believer as well as the community is directly tied to the new identity, which Paul now associates with belonging to a family as sons of God (v. 14). Christian behaviour, both individually and communally, is not only to reflect who believers are, but *whose* they are. Or as Morris puts it, "it is important that those who are Christ's live as those who are Christ's."[68] The reason for the believer's obligation to walk according to the Spirit is given in verse 13.[69] To live according to the flesh results in a certain death. Over against the certain death that results from living according to the flesh is the assurance that the one who lives according to the Spirit, by putting to death the deeds of the body, will live. It is important to note that Paul specifically speaks of the *praxeis*, "deeds" of the body rather than works of the flesh. The word relates to actions and practices that result from our beliefs. Paul probably used the word in order to emphasize that right belief must show itself in right, concrete, and tangible behavior. It is in so doing that the believer demonstrates that he or she is being led by the Spirit. The decisiveness with which believers are to deal with the deeds of the flesh is conveyed in 8:13b—they are to put the deeds of the flesh to death, otherwise, they will die. The consistency with which they must do so is implicit in the use of the present tense of the verb that Paul uses for "putting to death." So also is the inevitability of the death that results, should they fail to obey, conveyed by the periphrastic future, "you must die."

Believers are to put to death the deeds of the body, and in so doing be led by the Spirit. In verse 14, the particle *for* suggests that the verse is a clarification as well as a restatement of verse 13. The crucial questions to be asked are: What does it mean to be led by the Spirit? What are its implications for holiness? The verb '*agontai*,' Burke notes, has been translated as "driven by" the Spirit (cf. 1 Cor. 2:12) and is the language of 'enthusiasts,' such as we find in Corinth.[70] However, the lexical evidence is lacking because nowhere is this verb translated to 'drive.'[71]

Being led by the Spirit is not restricted to a few ecstatics, but is to be seen as a typical experience of all God's children. In its present context, it has to do with the whole idea of either walking according to the flesh or in accordance with the Spirit. It is about holiness in daily living. It is not to be construed as a sporadic or occasional event but a lifestyle of daily submission of the believer to the Spirit, the resultant effect of which is a continual putting to death of the misdeeds of the flesh. It is something continuous, affecting all the operations of the believer's activities throughout every moment of his/her life.

The leading provided by the Holy Spirit, contrary to the popular understanding of the passage, is not just a matter of the Spirit providing guidance to the believer or providing help in decision-making.[72] Rather, it has moral undertones in as much as the Spirit-led-sons-of God are obligated to put to death the flesh daily. It has but one goal in view—the saving from sin, the leading unto holiness. Hendriksen's view on the "leading by the Spirit" is right on target. He writes:

What then does the leading of the Spirit—to change from the passive to the active voice —actually mean? It means sanctification. It is the constant, effective, and beneficent influence which the Holy Spirit exercises within the hearts and lives of God's children, enabling them more and more to crush the power of indwelling sin and to walk in the way of God's commandments freely and cheerfully.[73]

So also is Ferguson's succinct explanation of what it means to be led by the Spirit. He writes:

But the leading of the Spirit of which Paul speaks has a very clear and definite content here. It is connected intimately with the help the Spirit is said to give in verse 13, to 'put to death the misdeeds of the body.' The guidance the Spirit provides is that of clear-cut opposition to sin. To claim to experience the ministry of the Spirit of adoption and yet to dally with sin is to be gravely deceived. The Spirit of adoption is the same person as the Spirit of holiness of whom Paul had earlier spoken (Rom. 1:4). His presence brings a new attitude to sin. Where that new attitude is present, he is present.[74]

Thus, the real test for the believer is the willingness to respond to the directions of the Spirit that dwells within, particularly when the Spirit directs attention to specific behavioural patterns that Paul here describes as deeds of the body. Although Paul will get to practical instructions later on in his letter, he simply leaves the misdeeds to the convicting work of the Spirit at this point. The important point to note here, Schreiner suggests, is that those who are led or governed by the Spirit are the children of God, or God's eschatological people.[75] The argument in this section reaches a climax in 15-17, where Paul speaks of adoption.[76] Paul's argument can thus be summed up as follows. Christians have received the Spirit of adoption (v. 15a), in that they cry "Abba, Father" (v. 15b). In verse 16, Paul speaks about the witness of the Spirit.[77] This is followed by the assertion that believers are heirs of God and joint-heirs with Christ. The ethical implications are the main concern here, and is well summed up by L H. Marshall,

> The ethical implications of Adoption are obvious. A 'son of God' must behave in a manner worthy of his august descent, and only those who behave so truly are truly "sons" . . . . only as men behave like God can they really prove themselves to be the sons of God.[78]

Thus, it is right to suggest that Spirit-filled living entails that believers, both communally and individually, must be committed to reflecting God's holiness in daily living. Several things are to be noted concerning verse 17. It points the reader back to the language of adoption that is found in verse 15. As a result of adoption, believers are now children of God through the witness of the Spirit (v. 16). But more than that, believers are heirs together with Christ. Here, one could see the eschatological tension of 'already/not yet' that is characteristic of Paul's theology. Heir-ship looks forward to the future. Paul's solidaric emphasis is equally striking. This is expressed in terms of the relationship between the believing community and Christ. Paul speaks of "being heirs together with Christ," "suffering together," and "being glorified together with Christ." Finally, the verse prepares the reader for the rest of the chapter as Paul expounds on believers' sufferings and the possibilities of victory. Believers can endure sufferings with fortitude because of the hope of glory and the assurance of a completed redemption. However terrible present suffering might be, Paul argues, it is "incomparable with the glory which shall be revealed in us."

Verses 18-25

18. For I consider that the sufferings of this present time are not worthy to be compared with the glory that is to be revealed to us. 19. For the anxious longing of the creation waits eagerly for the revealing of the sons of God. 20. For the creation was subjected to futility, not of its own will, but because of Him who subjected it, in hope 21. that the creation itself also will be set free from its slavery to corruption into the freedom of the glory of the children of God. 22. For we know that the whole creation groans and suffers the pains of childbirth together until now. 23. And not only this, but also we ourselves, having the first fruits of the Spirit, even we ourselves groan within ourselves, waiting eagerly for our adoption as sons, the redemption of our body. 24. For in hope we have been saved, but hope that is seen is not hope; for why does one also hope for what he sees? 25. But if we hope for what we do not see, with perseverance we wait eagerly for it.

Paul provides a vital perspective that those who are led by the Spirit discover. "In view of the concealed nature of our adoption, we understand that our existence as Spirit-filled Christians, must include the sufferings of the present time.[79] Paul shows that the believer is living in a mixed age. Though set free, believers still live in a world tarnished by sin. Believers are not delivered from the sufferings of the present time as some today believe. Neither should we conclude that a believer's suffering is due to lack of faith. Paul says, "For I consider that the sufferings of this present time are not worthy to be compared with the glory that is to be revealed in us."

Paul compares the present suffering with the eschatological glory that is to be revealed in rather than to believers. The comparison is not about value.

Although Paul's primary concern is not to answer the question of why the righteous suffer, he, nevertheless, shows that sanctification or holiness does not provide immunity from trials and sufferings. Instead, it is that which enables the Christians to maintain an attitude of trust and confidence in God in the midst of life's circumstances. Thus, life in the Spirit is that of blessed assurance that God is in control. Amid present suffering, believers wait patiently and confidently for full salvation—the revelation of God's glory.

In Rom. 8:1-17, it has been shown that holiness or life in the Spirit is characterised both by freedom and responsibility. From this point on, Paul portrays the sanctified life as that of hope in the midst of sufferings. He shows that a life that is lived under the guidance of the Spirit is that which, living in a world of evil, can experience the sufferings of this life, and can relate to perplexities and hardships that are a part of human experience, all with steadfast faith and sure hope.

Doubtless, what Paul said had very real meaning for community of believers in Rome, and it has equal meaning for Christians of the twenty-first century. Paul's point is clear. Sanctification does not provide immunity from suffering. Instead, suffering is to be understood as a normal part of Christian experience. Whatever the cause of believers' suffering, they can endure them when they remember the glory of the life to come. Paul is thinking about a finished redemption, of our sharing in the glory of Christ in eternity. What steadying assurance this should give to those who suffer from the ravages of disease such as AIDS, to those who are victims of injustice and wickedness, to persecuted saints in many places, and to all Christians who have felt the hard blows of inescapable tragedy and cruel circumstance and crushing affliction.

In vv. 19-22, Paul goes on to expand on the present suffering of v. 18, arguing that it is not only humans who are involved but also the non human creation. The whole creation, Paul contends, has suffered from the blight of sin in human experience and in some way longs for the consummation of humanity's redemption. The whole creation feels the separation, alienation, and corruption that human sin has entailed and seeks to be free from it.[80] It earnestly looks forward to "the manifestation of the sons of God." Paul's language is full of poetic imagery. Here is a cosmic drama. The creation was subjected to vanity, not voluntarily, but because of the will of God. It felt the impact of Adam's fall into sin. Nonetheless, it was subjected "in hope." It also shares in the hope of redemption. But the time will come when the creation will be "delivered from the bondage of corruption into the glorious liberty of the children of God." The groaning of creation indicates something of the greatness of Christ's redemptive work. For Paul, salvation is the restoration not just of individuals or the isolated spirit, but also of God's entire creation. The renewal of all things is both connected and anchored on human renewal in the same manner as human degradation is connected with all things. Is Paul concerned with the environment? Or asked differently, "do these verses speak to ecological issues?" Certainly, yes. But Kaylor's words on these verses are very helpful:

> Paul's speaking of creation's groaning in this passage is not intended to create sympathy for creation, nor is its primary intent to exhort humans to be more responsible for the environment. Both those concerns may be worthy applications of Paul's theology to the present ecological crisis, and persons concerned about the environment may welcome the assistance of the apostle in responding faithfully to that crisis. But Paul's intent was not to discuss the problems of creation as such; it was to focus upon the sufferings of the present time, and especially upon the question of whether those sufferings nullify the hope he has for the future.[81]

Paul carries his argument one step further in v. 23: "And not only this, but also we ourselves, having the first fruits of the Spirit, even we ourselves groan within ourselves, waiting eagerly for our adoption as sons, the redemption of our body." Moreover, Paul says that we Christians, who have the first fruits (*aparche*) of the Sprit—that is, the first installment — have our groaning for the fulfillment of our redemption. In other words, we yearn for the fruition of our adoption in the redemption of the body. For believers the new age has already begun and its blessings belong to us. But we eagerly wait for the consummation, the redemption of our body. [82] This is indeed the hope of that Paul speaks about in verses 24 and 25.

Such hope is central in our Christian salvation. "In hope we were saved." Hope is not daydreaming; it is disciplined waiting. It caries the idea of expectation and confidence. There s something better yet. It is more wonderful than our finite minds can grasp, more glorious than imagination can conceive. It is a bright vision that leads us forward and imparts steadfastness and perseverance regardless of trial or disappointment or failure. Because of our hope of heaven itself, we are made strong to endure.

> 26. And in the same way the Spirit also helps our weakness; for we do not know how to pray as we should, but the Spirit Himself intercedes for us with groanings too deep for words; 27. and He who searches the hearts knows what the mind of the Spirit is, because He intercedes for the saints according to the will of God.

Verses 26-27 provide further description of Sprit-filled living. It is a life of prayer. But it involves more than human abilities and eloquence. The Holy Spirit is intimately involved. He is the believers' helper—the believers' prayer partner! What a staggering truth! What a comfort! In the complex experiences of life, we are often confounded, bewildered, and blinded—confused about duty, about affliction, and about the raging power of evil in the world order. And, therefore, we do not know how to pray for ourselves, for others, and for the cause of redemption. But the Holy Spirit "helps our weaknesses," that is, he helps us in our weakness—weaknesses of the present age. Paul uses here a graphic word for help (*sunantilambano*). It means that the Spirit takes hold of our difficulty face to face at the same time. Thus the Holy Spirit helps us as we pray. Our prayer becomes His prayer. We do not understand the things for which we should pray. But the Spirit himself (not "itself") intercedes for us with groanings too deep for words. He intercedes for us with agonizing earnestness. He knows how to translate our requests into acceptable petitions before the Father because he has perfect understanding of God's will and he is in perfect harmony with God's will. He (God) who searches our hearts knows the mind of the Spirit (v. 27). When He searches our hearts, He does not find the imperfect groanings but the mind of the Spirit. Thus, the key thing in prayer is not intelligence or eloquence but oneness or participation with the Spirit.

Verses 28-30

28. And we know that God causes all things to work together for good to those who love God, to those who are called according to His purpose. 29. For whom He foreknew, He also predestined to become conformed to the image of His Son, that He might be the first-born among many brethren; 30. and whom He predestined, these He also called; and whom He called, these He also justified; and whom He justified, these He also glorified.

These verses portray the Spirit-filled life as that which is filled with assurance. What Paul provides is further basis of assurance in the midst of suffering. In spite of suffering and weakness, in spite of persecution or hardship, or in spite of anything and everything, God is in control. For those who love him and who are committed to his purpose, he makes all things "work together for good,"or at least is working powerfully for good. In other words, a gracious providence overrules all of life. That providence is the outworking of God's will for his children. The emphasis needs to be put where Paul placed it. In this whole section Paul was thinking about suffering. As such, Paul suggests that suffering can help to prepare believers for their life with God by making them more Christlike. He can turn sickness and misfortune, hardship and persecution, sorrow and death, tension and conflict, all of life's experiences into a means of blessing for those who keep on loving him, for those who want his purpose to be fulfilled in them.

V. 29 takes Paul's argument on sanctification further. It presents sanctification as God's eternal purpose. He purposed that we should be "conformed to the image of his Son," that is, that we should grow more and more in the likeness of Christ. One cannot claim to be confident of being loved and called by God without being challenged about what he/she is in his/her own life. Sanctification is not merely to be set apart. He set us apart to be like His Son. The word "image" *eikon* is an important word for Paul.[83] Its usage here is close to 2 Cor. 3:18. Paul is here saying that believers will be conformed to the nature of Christ. Although this event is commenced in the present age, it belongs decisively to the future; and in the future it will be consummated. Those whom God foreordained unto eternal life, he called; those whom he called, he also justified; those whom he justified, he also glorified. Paul declares the fact of glorification as though it had already taken place. It is of course still in the future, but it is absolutely certain of fulfillment. Here, then, we have the climax of God's redemptive work in Jesus Christ and through his Spirit. God's purpose is that the sons of God shall be like the Son of God. His sovereign purpose and power are the guarantee of future glorification. The God of grace is the God of purpose, and the God of purpose is the God of power.[84] Bowens sums up these verses very well: "If we are not beginning to be like Him now, no confidence about our predestination nor hope of future glory are of any value. Our predestination is to be like Christ; only those who are like Him will share His glory."[85]

### Verses 31-39

31. What then shall we say to these things? If God is for us, who is against us? 32. He who did not spare His own Son, but delivered Him up for us all, how will He not also with Him freely give us all things? 33. Who will bring a charge against God's elect? God is the one who justifies; 34. who is the one who condemns? Christ Jesus is He who died, yes, rather who was raised, who is at the right hand of God, who also intercedes for us. 35. Who shall separate us from the love of Christ? Shall tribulation, or distress, or persecution, or famine, or nakedness, or peril, or sword? 36. Just as it is written, "For Thy sake we are being put to death all day long; 37. But in all these things we overwhelmingly conquer through Him who loved us. 38. For I am convinced that neither death, nor life, nor angels, nor principalities, nor things present, nor things to come, nor powers, 39. nor height, nor depth, nor any other created thing, shall be able to separate us from the love of God, which is in Christ Jesus our Lord.

The passage caps Paul's exposition of the righteousness of God. It is important to briefly review his argument up to this point. He has shown the guilt of humanity because of the universality of sin and because of God's wrath against sin (1:18-3:20). He has set forth the truth about justification by faith and the way of salvation by grace (3:21-5:21).

Furthermore, he has shown the need for sanctification and portrayed the new life in Christ as that of freedom and responsibility (6:1-8:17). Now he comes to the climax of his argument in a burst of jubilant assurance that nothing can defeat the purpose of God's grace, because nothing can separate the believer from the love of God in Jesus Christ our Lord. On this basis, we have security.

There are several questions in this section. In v. 31 Paul asks: "What shall we then say to these things?" Perhaps, by "these things" Paul is referring back to all that he had been saying about God's salvation and God's sovereign purpose of grace for his children. However, it seems more likely that Paul is pointing more definitely to "the sufferings of this present time," to the temptations and trials of life, to the infirmities and hardships that are common to experience. What can Christians say, what assurance can they have, in the light of life's perplexities and perils? Paul gives three answers. The first one is, God is for us, or God is on our side. Believers are not without opponents. It is the assurance of God's help and presence that makes the difference. No greater security is needed, available or provided. The question, "If God be for us, who can be against us?" is rhetorical. It does not imply doubt. Paul put it that way for emphasis. Since God is for us, it makes no difference who is against us. The Roman gods were fickle, sometimes for, and sometimes against their adherents. The overwhelming and incontrovertible evidence that God is for us is provided in v. 32. He spared not His own Son but gave him up for us all. It is the demonstration of the reality of God being with us. The Christ event settles it decisively that God is for us. God saw humanity's need— guilt in sin, helplessness, and utter ruin because of sin. In response to this need and because of his grace, God went to the extreme of giving his own Son to be the propitiation for sins. If God was willing to go this far, "how shall he not with him also freely give us all things?" Specifically, he will give us the full benefit of his redemption to guarantee for us an abundant entrance into his everlasting kingdom. In the light of what God has done, we can have no question that his attitude toward us is one of redemptive longing, infinite love, and compassionate mercy. The resources of God have been expended to the point of the cross of Christ. Therefore, we can be sure that God's investment in our salvation will not come short of fruition.

Paul asks a second question: "Who shall lay any thing to the charge of God's elect?" In other words, who can make any indictment against the Christian? No indictment can stand because God is the one who justifies. The Christian has been justified by faith. He has received forgiveness for sin. He is a trophy of divine grace and has a standing before God that no one can alter. Since our sins are against God, and he has justified us freely "by his grace through the redemption that is in Christ Jesus," there can be no one to bring a charge against us.

We have the same idea repeated in the question, "Who is he that condemns?" There was condemnation for sin. We deserved the wrath of God. But Christ died in our behalf. Through him we have received the atonement. He was made sin for us that we might be made righteousness. This is an echo of Rom. 8 1: "There is therefore no condemnation for those who are in Christ Jesus." The apostle goes on to declare the great central facts of Christ's redemptive work. He died, he arose from the dead, he ascended to the right hand of God, and he makes intercession for us as our great High Priest. Through his death he became the curse for us. Through his resurrection he proved the validity of his sacrifice and the reality of his power over sin and death. His ascension reveals his majesty and declares his sovereign power. As our Advocate, he pleads the merits of his sacrifice for all our sins, past, present, and future. Because he ever lives to intercede, he is able to save unto the uttermost (Heb. 7:25).

Once again, for argument and emphasis, Paul asks a third and final question: "Who shall separate us from the love of Christ?" In verse 39 we have "the love of God." The love of Christ and the love of god are the same in meaning. Paul calls the list of the severest trials: tribulation, distress, persecution, famine, nakedness, peril, and sword. The apostle knew in his own experience the reality of these trials. Christians throughout the centuries have been called on to endure them. They do not separate us from Christ's love. They may separate us from wealth and health, from family and friends, from comfort and ease. But they can have absolutely no effect upon the unchangeable love of God. Quoting from Psalm 44:22, Paul says that these trials are like an experience of slow torture. It seems that we are being "killed all the day long," that we are "accounted as sheep for the slaughter"—all for God's sake. But such suffering does not mean that God's love has changed or that anything has separated us from it.

Instead, all these trials give opportunity for God's love in Christ to demonstrate its power. In all these things we can be "more than conquerors through him that loved us." Paul is saying that we can keep on living victoriously. We can be conquerors with a wide margin! We can do it through Christ, whose love never fails. The chapter concludes with Paul's triumphant affirmation of faith. He traverses the entire range of experience to declare that nothing can separate us from God's love in Christ. Nothing in daily experience—"neither death, nor life"; nothing in the hierarchy of invisible powers, either good or evil—"nor angels, nor principalities, nor powers"; nothing in time or space—"nor things present, nor things to come, nor height or depth"; nothing in all creation—"nor any other creature." Nothing shall ever "be able to separate us from the love of God, which is in Christ Jesus our Lord." What a blessed assurance. Such is the life in the Spirit, the new life in Christ, **the life of that has been transformed by grace.**

What Paul has written in these verses ought to answer every question one can raise about the ultimate outcome of faith in Christ. It is clear from these verses, and the chapter as a whole, that Paul thought that believers should be sure of their final salvation. But there is more in this passage than the divine affirmation of spiritual security. There is also a challenge to Christians to live out the victorious life made possible by the Spirit, demonstrate to the world the faith, courage, and joy that ought to result from the conviction that they are the holy people of God to whom there is no condemnation.

## Conclusion

In concluding this chapter, one must return to the question of what Spirit-filled living is all about. Is it to be construed strictly in terms of speaking in tongues and manifestation of the spiritual gifts as valid and necessary as those may be? The answer is, undoubtedly, no. It is much more! Paul sees the Holy Spirit as the moral force for daily living. The Christian's present experience of Christ, is through the Spirit, and the Spirit is the power of the Christian's ethical life. The indwelling of the power of the Spirit is to transform the human being through Jesus Christ, God's Son. There is not just one ministry of the Holy Spirit described here by Paul, but many. The Spirit is involved in our salvation (8:1-2) and in our sanctification (8:3). The Spirit initiates, guides and empowers our actions, so that the righteousness God requires is fulfilled (8:9-14). He also assures us of our sonship, as the Spirit of adoption (8:15). The Holy Spirit is the answer to the problem of the Christian's "body of death," a body dominated by sin and dead with respect to producing any work which is righteous, according to the definition of the Law of God. Romans 8 deals with the ministry of the Holy Spirit pertaining to the salvation and sanctification, communally as well as personally. It is in Romans 12 that Paul approaches the subject of the ministry of the Holy Spirit for service and ministry when the subject of spiritual gifts is addressed. Thus, it may be concluded that there is nothing in the chapter that suggests that the believer, because of his or her experience of sanctification no longer needs to "receive the Holy Spirit." The second conclusion logically follows from the preceding. Sanctification is not to be confused with the baptism with the Holy Spirit. It is possible to distinguish between the two by comparing Rom. 8:1-17 with other passages in the Pauline corpus. The notion of the Holy Spirit only as "power for service," as Pentecostals emphasise, is not entirely correct. The Holy Spirit is God's provision for holy living in the life of the Christian.

Attention must equally be paid to the 'already' and 'not yet' which is so often decisive in Paul's argument and also very prominent in this passage as well as throughout the balance of Romans 8. It is impossible to live the Christian life in the power of the flesh; it is possible only in the strength of the Holy Spirit. The unbeliever can only live according to the flesh by which he/she is enslaved. The Christian has a choice. The Christian can live in the realm of the flesh or in the realm of the Spirit. He/She will live in one of these two worlds. He/She will walk in accordance with one of these two ways—the way of the flesh or the way of the Spirit. From Paul's point of view, there is no good reason to walk according to the flesh and every reason to walk according to the Spirit. As the discussion of this chapter has shown, Paul's ethic grows out of his theology. Justification is to lead to sanctification. Spirit-filled living without a corresponding victorious life would be anachronistic at least.

Moreover, as the second half of the chapter shows, to be joined with Christ does not make life easier. Yet in the midst of all sufferings believers are sure of victory as they rely on the Spirit who prays for and with them.

The Gospel is a message of victory, not only in view of what lies ahead in the future, but already in view of the experience of the Christian community of which the individual is a constituent member. Finally, I must say that there is more in this chapter than could be fathomed in a lifetime, much less in a few pages. What is significant is that the chapter commends itself to us lo live our lives by the power of the Holy Spirit, basking in God's love and being daily conformed to the image of His Son.

# Chapter 5
## Holiness: Beyond Romans 6-8

The task I set for myself in this study was to examine Paul's theology of sanctification in Rom. 6 through 8. In doing so, I set to (1) show that the three chapters are thematically connected and (2) demonstrate that Paul's understanding of holiness in Rom. 6-8 is consonant with his teachings elsewhere. With regards to the first objective, it has been clearly shown that Paul's overarching thought in the three chapters was holiness. Paul's exhortation is for the community to live according to its position and status in Christ. Having been transformed in Christ, the community is now to live according to the premises provided in those chapters. A life of holiness is that which is transformed living—free from the bondage of sin. Paul, in these chapters puts the responsibility for living a holy life squarely on the Christian community. It is not just a "stop trying and trusting" business. Believers are to yield themselves as slaves to righteousness, leading unto sanctification (6:23). Holiness is both freedom and slavery—freedom from sin and freedom (slavery) to serve God. God has made adequate provisions for holiness but believers are responsible for using those provisions. Furthermore, it has been argued that the freedom Paul talks about is not merely a freedom from judicial consequences, but a freedom unto holiness. At the same time it is freedom that comes with obligations. It is not a freedom from God but for God. Sanctification, it has been contended, must always accompany justification.

The discussion on Rom. 6 clearly shows that grace is powerful enough to produce new life in Christians, so that instead of living in sin they will want to walk in newness of life. In Chapter 7, holiness is shown by Paul to be a life of freedom from the bondage of the law. It is not a life of unending struggle. The whole argument reaches its climax in chapter 8 where Paul makes it plain that freedom both from sin and the law are made possible only through the power of the Holy Spirit. It is clear that holiness is based on the graciousness of God, and effected by the Spirit. Holiness, as envisioned by Paul in these chapters is not something to be achieved by obedience to the law. Instead, as Paul ably demonstrates in Chapter 8, it is by the enabling power of the Spirit. The Holy Spirit stands in close possible relation with the ethical life of the believers. Being possessors of the Spirit (Rom. 8) does not excuse believers from seeking sanctification. By the use of participationist language such as 'buried with Him,' 'baptised into His death,' 'raised with Him,' in these chapters, Paul presents a view of the Christian life as one that is wholly lived out in Christ by the power of the Holy Spirit. Chapters 6-8 basically describe an interim ethics of the Christian community as it awaits the consummation of all things. As such, Paul's understanding of holiness reflects both his communal and eschatological understanding of the church. It is to be noted in these chapters that the believers' holiness stems from their relationship with God through Christ, and is lived by the enabling power of the Holy Spirit.

How does the understanding of holiness in these chapters parallel Paul's view of holiness in his other writings? An exhaustive answer goes beyond the scope of this book. Nevertheless, it is clear that it does. It is to this we now turn our attention. First, it is important to note that the same indicative-imperative schema which was argued in connection Rom. 6-8 pervades Paul's other letters. By means of the indicatives and imperatives, not only do the relational and ethical aspects of sanctification become clear, one may make a distinction in Paul's thought concerning justification and sanctification. For example, the people who were justified, were the ones called "saints" in Rom. 1:7. They were God's holy people by virtue of their relationship with Him through Christ. They *have died to sin*, a concept, which, we have argued must have had its expression both in their conversion and baptism. In that regard, one may suggest that there is an aspect of sanctification, which, although it does not constitute conversion is simultaneous with it. Nevertheless, as we have argued, they are exhorted to make progress and press forward. This is the thrust of the imperatives. Usually, Paul expresses the progress both with the aorist and present tenses,[86] which suggest definitive as well as progressive aspects of sanctification. The indicatives and imperatives are to be seen as being together in equilibrium rather being in fusion.

**Romans 12-15**

Without doubt, Paul's comments in these closing chapters of Romans cover a wide range of topics. Yet it is evident that Paul is still preoccupied with the concerns that he has earlier expressed in beginning chapters. In this section Paul particularly focuses on how the righteousness of God should be reflected both in the Christian and wider community. In Rom.12:1-2, Paul summarily states the ethical implications as well as the response that Christians are to make in view of God's mercies, of which Paul has spoken at length in the preceding. In this section he begins to describe in practical details how Christians should live out their new relationship with Christ. Once again, we must remember that the people to whom Paul is about to address are those who have been justified through faith (5:1), "set free from sin" (6:18), "released from the law" (7:6) and made "alive" in Christ (8:10). The particle *therefore* with which Paul opens the passage does not only connect the reader with the preceding eleven chapters but looks forward to affirm that justification should lead to transformation. It is important to note that, in the same way that he has done in Rom. 6-8, Paul employs the imperatives. Although with slight modification in language[87], in the same manner as in 6:13, Paul commands the believers to "present *their* bodies a living and holy sacrifice" (12:2). He goes further with a prohibition for the Roman Christians "not to be conformed to this world." Instead, they should be "transformed by the renewing of *their* mind." Paul here calls upon the Roman Christians to make a decisive act of yielding themselves to God. A second significant point to note is the communal nature of Paul's command. Richard Hays sums it well. He writes:

> *The church is a countercultural community of discipleship, and this community is the primary addressee of God's imperatives.* The biblical story focuses on God's design for forming a covenant *people.* Thus, the primary sphere of moral concern is not the character of the individual but the corporate obedience of the church. Paul's formulation in Romans 12:1-2 encapsulates the vision: "Present your bodies [*somata*, plural] as a living sacrifice [*thysian*, singular], holy and well-pleasing to God. . . . And do not be conformed to this age, but be transformed by the renewing of your mind" The

community, in its corporate life, is called to embody an alternative order that stands as a sign of God's redemptive purposes in the world. . . . The coherence of the New Testament's ethical mandate will come into focus only when we understand that mandate in *ecclesial* terms, when we seek God's will not by asking first, "What should I do," but "What should *we* do?"[88]

In Romans 13:14 Paul admonishes the believers to "put on the Lord Jesus," a phrase that sums up all the instructions and exhortations that Paul has given in the preceding verses. In putting on the Lord Jesus the believers will make no provision for the flesh to gratify its desires. Christian behavior is based on Christ Himself, He being the center of the Christians' life and thought. Paul's words re-echo 12:2. To "put on", or "be clothed" with the Lord Jesus as the word means, parallels Paul's command to be "transformed by the renewing of your mind."[89]

As a summary of Rom. 12-15 the following should be noted with respect to sanctification or holy living. First, the gospel has practical results that are seen in the way believers behave (Rom.12:1-21). Second, holy living, which should characterize believers, depends on the power of the Holy Spirit. As the new people of God and members of God's new family, Christians possess the Holy Spirit who guides, helps, and assists them to live in a way that pleases God. Although Paul did not say so explicitly in these chapters, he did not need to do so, having already done so in chapter 8. In the freedom that the Holy Spirit brings, the choice is always there as never before under the slavery of sin. Third, transformed living is not an individual business. It involves our individual relationship with others. It involves our daily relationship with others such as other members of our biological family; other members of Christ's new family outside our own denominational circles (see especially12:3-13 and 14:1-15:13); and other members of the society who are still outside the family of God (12:14-13:7).

## 1 and 2 Corinthians[90]

Clearly and unmistakably in the Corinthian correspondence, Paul insists on holiness of heart and righteousness of life. The Corinthians have become the people of God by being "sanctified in Christ Jesus," that is, by being "set apart" for God. All who have been brought to faith in Christ are qualified as *hagioi* (holy ones or saints; cf. 1 Cor. 16:4; 2 Cor. 1:4; 13:12; 8:4; 9:1, 12.), and the community can be described as the temple of God (1 Cor. 3:17).

As the recipients of God's grace in Christ, the members of the believing community are the people whom Christ purchased for the sake of God's glory (1 Cor. 6:20). As God's rightful possession which is evidenced both through indwelling of the Spirit and the redemptive work of Christ who is our sanctification, believers are to glorify God. To glorify God includes making him known. Those who do not know Christ are incapable of giving glory to God (Cf. Rom. 3: 23). However, as the behavioural aberrations among the Corinthians clearly show, the capacity to glorify God may or may not be actualized, and it is on this that Paul's concern is focussed in several passages (cf. 1 Cor. 5:1-13; 6:1-20). In such passages Paul not only contrasts the pattern of behavior of the Corinthians with that of their surrounding society but clearly does so to show that the state to which believers have been called imposes a demand that must be met if the title of "saint" is not be evacuated of all meaning. It should entail observable behaviour, and as 1 Corinthians particularly reveals, this is often lacking in a community whose spirituality and elevation of wisdom are not reflected in ethical attitudes.

They are also called to be saints, a phrase that echoes Ex. 19:5-6. As such, Paul contended that the gospel issued in transformed lives and that salvation in Christ is incomplete without Christlike attitudes and behaviours.[91] Paul viewed the Christian community in Corinth to be God's eschatological people, a view that Paul argues must determine its lifestyle in the present age.[92] In 2 Cor. 7:1, Paul, as a summary exhortation of the preceding verses (6:14-18), enjoins the Corinthians "let us cleanse ourselves." Including himself by the use of *eautous* "ourselves" he summoned the Corinthian church to cease from unacceptable relationships with iniquity, the powers of darkness, Belial, unbelievers, and idols. This is a call to communal holiness, which is both relational and ethical. Paul had acknowledged earlier (1 Cor. 6:9-11a) that the Corinthians had been washed, a reference to their conversion-initiation experience. It is thus right to suggest that the whole exhortation in 2 Cor. 6:14-7:1 stands in relation to the process aspect of holiness, as indicated by the present tense of the participle. Therefore, cleansing, in this passage has to do with a proper use of the temple, the dwelling-place of the Holy Spirit and through which God is to be glorified (Cf. 1 Cor. 6:15-20).

Furthermore, in 2 Cor. 11:2, Paul uses the imagery of bethrothal that is in conformity with Jewish customs in his appeal to the Corinthians. In the Old Testament, Israel is frequently depicted as bethrothed to Yahweh. Paul now thinks of the Christian community, specifically, the Corinthian congregation as the pure bride of Christ, Christ as the bridegroom, and of himself as one who is to present the bride to her husband.[93] Paul uses the marriage relationship—the complete separation of a man and a woman from all others only to each other —as a picture of the relationship that is supposed to exist between God and his people. In this one picture, we see clearly the separation aspect of holiness emphasised. As the bride is separated from all others to her husband alone, so the people of God are separated not only from every form of defilement but to him. By accepting the gospel, the Corinthians had committed themselves totally to Christ, but they would be united fully with him only at his Second Coming. In the interval it was Paul's responsibility to ensure that they lived up to their engagement implicit in their baptism.[94] Although betrothed, according to the Jewish law, the violation of a betrothed virgin was no less serious than if the marriage had already been consummated. In the same way that God was jealous for the undivided loyalty of Israel, so also is Paul with the Corinthians. Given this background, Paul's exhortation to the Corinthians in 1 Cor. 11:2f. becomes clearer. As people who are incorporated into Christ, they must live as befits their status.

### Galatians

In Galatians one finds the same pattern that is found in Rom. 6-8. It is commonly agreed that the law, particularly circumcision, is an important issue in Galatians. But Paul does not directly address the issue of circumcision until chapter 5 where he sets the issue of circumcision against the Spirit-filled life.[95] In Gal. 5:24, Paul apparently links the crucifixion of the flesh with the belonging-ness to Christ. It is conceivable, therefore, to think about the crucifixion of the flesh and its desires with the crucifixion of Christ. Paul is expressing the same idea as in Rom 6:6. The "old self" has been crucified with Christ. This views a change that has already taken place. The death of the flesh, is not, however, something that works automatically. It is an event that must be appropriated by faith. It is probably no accident, nor is without significance, therefore, that here Paul states in the active voice what elsewhere he puts in the passive: "Now those belong to Christ *have crucified* the flesh with its passions and desires"(Gal. 5:24). The aorist points to a completed action in the past and might most naturally refer to conversion.[96] He is speaking of an act of will on the part of those who belong to Christ. It is therefore not correct to see this just as a theological statement referring to one's position in Christ[97] but as something that occurs in the Christian consciousness. They have renounced fellowship with sin whose seat is the "flesh" (sarx).[98] This has sometimes been understood as the believer's experience at baptism.[99] Although this may be possible, it is not explicit in the present text. Such interpretation seems forced. The apostle probably has in view the free moral decision by believers who belong to Christ. In conversion, they have made a conscious decision to follow the Lord. They have responded to God's saving grace in Christ. They have been regenerated, and now, they say a radical "No" to sin and thus pass judgment on the whole of their previous life. Hence Gal. 5:24 refers not to the mystery of baptism but to an ethical act on the part of Christians.[100] In verse 25, Paul's argument comes in a full circle. Although he does not use the imperative as he previously did in verse 16, his exhortation "let us also walk by the Spirit" has the same force, as succinctly stated by Parsons: "if the Spirit creates a new life-style (5:22-23) then it must be evidenced in the spiritual life of the believer. This is the moral corollary of to the indicative statement that precedes it—their conduct should be evidently governed by the Spirit of God."[101] In Galatians 5, in the same manner in Romans 8, Paul shows that the Holy Spirit stands in the closest possible relation to the ethical life of the believer.[102]

### Ephesians

Writing to the Ephesians Paul describes their former lifestyle as "following the course of this world, following the prince of the power of the air, the spirit that is now at work in the sons of disobedience." "Among these," he continued, "we all once lived in the passions of our flesh, following the desires of body and mind" (Eph. 2:2, 3). To Paul, it is obvious that a change has taken place in the lives of the Ephesians as a result of their response to the proclamation of the gospel. In Eph. 1:4 Paul links the reconciliation of the Ephesians with divine selection, and the goal is clearly stated: the presentation before God of the believers who are holy and blameless. In that these people were chosen as well as by virtue of their relationship to God through Christ, they were separated. The certainty of election is rooted "in Christ." Election is not for self-indulgence, but for a life that is "holy and blameless" and marked by love. The full implications of these terms will be spelled out beginning with chapter 4. In v.1, Paul implores the Ephesians "to walk worthy of the calling with you have been called." This is akin to "walking in the newness of life" (Rom. 6:4). God's holiness is to be replicated in the holiness of God's people. It becomes the responsibility of all believers to live in a manner worthy of God's calling by maintaining a clear separation between themselves and the society in which they lived. Specifically, Paul challenges the Ephesians to respond to the calling of God by fulfilling the three dimensions of the faith that he was about to elaborate: unity, diversity, and maturity. The problem of what the "old self" and "new self" imply has been previously dealt with in the discussion on Rom. 6. Nevertheless, it is important to note that Paul uses the same terminology of "old self" in Eph. 4:22-24. However one interprets the term, it is clear that for Paul, the ultimate goal of the Church is holiness, which includes both a "putting off" and cleansing. Paul urges the Ephesian Christians to "put on the new self, created to be like God in true righteousness and holiness (v. 24).

What Paul has in mind here is nothing short of the total change wrought within believers, a change that is reflected in their conduct. The practical expressions of the holy life that Paul has thus advocated are immediately listed in the verses that follow. Believers are to put off falsehood and speak truthfully (v. 25), be in control of their anger and deny the devil a foothold in their lives (vv. 26, 27), be honest in all relationships (v. 28), be devoid of unclean talk and unwise joking, but rather engage in conversations that are helpful and build others up (v. 29), be sensitive to the leadership of the Holy Spirit (v. 30), be without souring and , ill feelings (v.31) and be marked by tenderness that is inherent in holiness (v. 32). Paul's strong admonitions to a holy living continue in Eph. 5. Believers are to become imitators of God (v. 1). Paul uses the word *mimeitai*, a word the Ephesians would be able to relate to. Although Paul speaks of imitation in other passages (1 Cor. 4:16; 11:1; 2 Thess. 3:7, 9), the command here is unique as Paul speaks about imitating God. Here is what holiness is all about, "mirroring God." The imitation of God is influenced by our relationship with Him. As dearly loved lived children, The Ephesians should reciprocate their love to God by imitating Him.

Ephesians 5:26-27 brings the argument further. In the midst of exhortations to husbands and wives, Paul said, "loved the church and gave Himself up for her that he might sanctify her, having cleansed her by washing of water with the word, that He might present her to himself, a glorious church, not having spot, or wrinkle, or any such thing; but that it should be holy and blameless." In his comments on v.26, Winchester remarks:

> Just as Christ gave himself for the world that He might redeem it and that through His death might be saved, so did He give Himself for the Church that He might "sanctify it, having cleansed it." Both verbs are aorist in tense. The purpose for which He sanctifies and cleanses His Church is that he may "present" it to Himself "holy and without blemish." Only thus can it really be glorious in His sight and happy in His presence.[103]

It is evident that Paul's concern is to stress that when believers are presented before God, they are to be ethically pure and subject to no condemnation (Rom. 8:1). The life of holiness is again shown to be that which is transformed. In sum, the holiness that Paul presented to the Ephesians, as in his other writings, was the privilege and responsibility of those Christians to whom Paul wrote.

## Philippians

It has been noticed that Paul's letter to the Philippians is one of the warmest and most personal of Paul's letters. He begins the letter in the same way as Romans, 1 & 2 Corinthians, and Ephesians, addressing the recipients as saints, *hagioi*. In Philippians, Paul makes it clear that relationship with God demands a proper ethical response. Although the believers are *hagioi* "saints/holy ones", (1:1) at the very beginning of the letter, Paul makes it clear not only what the believers are but what they are to become. This is evident in his prayer in 1:9-11:

> And this I pray, that your love may abound still more and more in real knowledge and all discernment, so that you may approve the things that are excellent, in order to be sincere and blameless until the day of Christ; having been filled with the fruit of righteousness which comes through Jesus Christ, to the glory and praise of God..

Paul's prayers always provide an important clue to his theology. His prayer in this passage, as in others, is not for something that he expects or hopes to happen only in the future. Instead, he holds it forth as a present possibility, the effects of which are to continue through the believers' lives.[104] This is important as it shows the "already" and "not yet" aspects of Christian life. Although the Philippians have experienced the gift of the Spirit and enjoyed the benefits of salvation, they have been introduced to a work, that in one aspect (1:10) has as its conclusion the Day of Christ Jesus. Moreover, he prays that their love would abound more and more, and as it did, they would be able to discern what is of greatest importance. Paul's vocabulary deserves some attention. He uses words that have ethical implications. The word *elikrineis*, means to be sincere or blameless, pure, unmixed, possessing integrity and perfect purity of mind, heart, and conduct. One could thus argue that sincerity in human relations constitutes an essential aspect of the sanctified "transformed" life that we have been writing about. Further, Paul uses *aproskopoi*, which means to be without stumbling, without offense. It connotes purity. The import of this prayer inevitably leads to the conclusion that Paul believed in victory over sin and that perfect love is possible in this life. Stated differently, if purity is not possible in the present world, Paul's prayer is meaningless. "Purity and inoffensiveness are present moral and relational qualities to be maintained for the day of Christ."[105]

In Phil. 2:5, Paul begins the Christological hymn with an imperative, "Have this mind in you which was also in Christ Jesus" Two important observations need to be made. First is the word "mind", *phronein*. It signifies "the general mental attitude or disposition."[106] It "denotes rather a general disposition of mind than a specific act of thought directed at a given point."[107] There is a parallel with Rom. 8:6-7, where a related term (*phronema*) is used in the phrase "the mind of the Spirit." The implication is that the mind-set of the Spirit, which is the mind-set of Christ is to characterise the Philippian Christians. Second, it is important to note the communal aspect of the exhortation, suggested by "in you" (plural). Paul carries the argument further in Phil. 2:12-13, a passage that is not only significant because one finds a juxtaposition of the indicative and imperative, but also because it beautifully expresses the vital synergy between humans and the Spirit working through humans. Paul urges the believers to make the experience of salvation real in their everyday lives. Paul expresses their salvation in a corporate fashion; it belongs to all of them through the presence and activity of God in their midst. There is an "ought-ness" of what they should further become and how they should live. Yet it is God who makes it possible. It is a synergy—"neither the Spirit *nor* man acts alone."[108] As Walters correctly states, " the work involved on their part is an ongoing recognition of God's presence and activity, especially as it is manifested in the lives of those around them."[109] It is interesting to note that Paul uses the word *katergadzomai*, which means "work out," a word that he used several times in Rom. 7 (7:8, 13, 15, 17, 18, 20).[110] It assumes that there is something that is already in being, that is, already inside; the idea is to bring it out into view. There is nothing automatic about Spirit-filled living. Life by the Spirit is a relationship, both personal and communal, that must be cultivated and maintained. As Hawthorne correctly states, "it is clear that Christians individually and corporately have a very large part to play in the steady maintenance and strengthening of the new life which they have received from God as a result of Christ's death and resurrection."[111] The Philippians have entered a community whose existential attitudes sharply distinguish them from their surrounding society (14-16). As such, they must live up to their calling.

## Colossians

In his characteristic manner, in Colossians 1:21-23, Paul refers to the readers' former state of alienation and hostility; their reconciliation, its basis and result; and the necessity of their positive and continued response to the gospel which they have heard. In verse 22, Paul speaks of the reconciling effect that Christ's crucifixion had for those who had been estranged and hostile toward God. While on the one hand, Paul's reference to the death of Christ implied the justification of the Colossians, his use of the language of reconciliation highlights a change in relationship that is effected in reconciliation. Paul's readers who had previously no relationship with God are now related to Him through the death of Christ. Through Christ's work Christians may now anticipate being presented before God holy, blameless and irreproachable. The outcome of Christ's death for the Christian is not simply that they be presented in God's presence. Instead, the consequence of Christ's having established a new relationship between the believer and God is that when believers are presented they will be characterized as holy, blameless, and irreproachable. Without doubt, here holiness means more than a mere separation. It connotes ethical purity. The Colossians of whom Paul speaks and to whom he writes have been separated to God in the act of reconciliation. It is therefore quite absurd to either interpret or understand Paul's statement as saying that believers have been separated in order that they may be presented before God separated. Those who have been reconciled (Col. 2:12) are those who have been raised with Christ, whose life is Christ (Col. 3:1, 2), and who have put off the old self and put on the new. How then are believers to live while they await their final presentation before God? Paul spells out the ethical implications of the risen life in 3:1-14. They involve "putting to death" sins with a physical basis— "those things that belong to your members which are upon the earth; fornication, uncleanness, inordinate affection, evil concupiscence, and covetousness, which is idolatry" as well as the "putting off" of the attitudinal sins: "such as anger, wrath, malice, blasphemy, filthy communication out of your mouth" (vv. 5, 8). One cannot but notice that the verbs that Paul used for "putting to death" and "putting off" are aorist imperatives which suggests a decisive and crucial act. On the basis of the transforming events that the Colossians have experienced, both expressed by indicatives and in a manner reminiscent of Romans 6, Paul exhorts them to put on virtues that are consonant with their new status (vv. 5, 12).

## 1 and 2 Thessalonians

In addition to its attention to sanctification, 1 Thessalonians also offers instruction on the important theological topics of divine election and eschatology. There is no doubt that the Thessalonians are genuine Christians. Paul offers no criticisms of the Thessalonians' Christian conduct, even though they were recent converts from paganism. He made a special point of encouraging them to continue in the way of life they were already pursuing (1 Thess. 4:1, 9-10; 5:11, 4-5). The Thessalonians' conversions were not at all deficient. Once again, it is important to note that Paul was here addressing people who have entered into a new relationship of belonging to God in Christ through their salvation experience. They became imitators of the Lord (1:6); they are living pleasing to God (4:1); they love all the believers throughout Macedonia (4:10). It is unnecessary for such people to be more sanctified in a relational sense. The new relationship that is established between Christians and God in Christ involves in its act of initiation a transformation of the total person as well as a transferal of ownership of the entire person. However, those who belong to Christ need to mirror in their lives the character of their new master in an ever-increasing degree. For this reason, Paul prays that God will make holy all the believers.

Sanctification, as presented in 1 Thessalonians, in a similar manner to other letters, is intimately related to eschatology. In the letter, Paul deals with the problem, among others, of confusion about Christ's second coming. This is the basis of his exhortations to holiness in 3:12-4:2. A holy God calls His people to lives of holiness as the indispensable preparation for life in eternity with Him. Between Paul's two prayers for the sanctification of the Thessalonians, he appeals to them to allow God to sanctify them (3:12—4:12; 5:23-24). We shall now examine Paul's second prayer more closely.

In 1 Thess. 5:23a, Paul's prayer is that the God of peace Himself may sanctify you (*hagiasthai* is an aorist optative expressing an attainable wish). As in his other letters, Paul oscillates between an individualistic and corporate view of the members of the church. The second part of the verse suggests that the believers are blameless and that Paul is praying for the continuation of this situation. But the story doe not end there. There is another side to the coin. 1 Thess. 4:3-7 suggests there were some members with sexual problems (4:7) and that some were busybodies and idlers (4:11-13). Because of these persons Paul might pray "May God make you (plural) entirely holy." In other words, Paul is praying that the few persons of the group may become like the majority—ethically pure in their associations with the community. What one finds in 1 Thess. 4:3, 4, and 7 is Paul's discussion of concrete ways in which holiness is to be expressed, in a similar manner to Rom. 6:12-14. Believers are commanded to adhere to the given ethical practices precisely because they are grounded in the will of God to whom Christians as Christians must be obedient. Paul does not simply express the will of God for the believers in such concrete terms as he spelled out and then assert that they are solely responsible for compliance to the will of God. This obedience is their responsibility, but the possibility of success exists because God gives to the believers His Spirit. Here it is to be noted that Paul does not simply allude to Ezekiel 37:14 but modifies Spirit with "holy" probably to highlight the nature of the Spirit. Because the believers have received the Spirit who is holy, they may reasonably contemplate fulfilling the will of God which Paul has just set forth. This thought is continued in 2 Thessalonians. Paul insists that the God who called Christians also makes them worthy of His call and enables them to fulfill their "every good resolve" (2 Thess. 1:11-12). No-one can be "blameless in holiness" without the love that God's Spirit inspires and enables.

## The Pastoral Epistles

Although there is continuing debate on the authorship of the Pastoral Epistles,[112] it is clear that the pattern of holiness that is presented by Paul in Rom. 6-8 is also present. One of Paul's main concerns in 1 Timothy was to offset the influence of false teachers, hence Paul gives some instructions to Timothy. Paul states that the goal of instruction (both his and Timothy's) "is love from a pure heart" (1 Tim. 1:5). "Goal" here means an intended end and purpose. One of the unambiguous emphases in the Pastoral Epistles is that salvation involves a commitment to obedience to God. The believer is called to a belonging that involves the ethical transformation of his or her being. Those who are saved are both saved and called "to" a holy life, one in which there is no place for sin. Paul's use of the word *katharos* (pure) in the Pastorals is very instructive. He frequently links it with heart and conscience. A pure or clear conscience is more than one which is merely free from the guilt of sin. It is one that is transformed by the power and character of Christ.

As noted by Spross, even when the word purity is semantically ceremonial, "it is informed by the normative ethical understanding and entails moral renewal."[113] The deacon should hold the faith in a "pure conscience" 2 Tim. 3:9). Paul's "pure conscience" commends him to Timothy (2 Tim. 1:3); and his exhortation to young Timothy is that he, too, " follow righteousness, faith, charity [love], peace, with them that call on the Lord out of a pure heart" (2 Tim. 2:22). 2 Timothy 2:22 is significant for two reasons. First is the connection of the language of justification (righteousness) with that of sanctification (purity). Second is the use of the word *katharos*. The meaning supplied by the context is clearly an open, sincere, honest motivation in God's sight. Although good works do not save, the evidence of grace is a changed heart that brings forth good works (cf. Titus 2:11-14). Titus 2:14 gives a further definition of cleanness, in the midst of a block of ethical teaching that Paul gave to Titus. Paul introduces Christ the Savior, as he so often does. He is the one " who gave himself for us, that he might redeem us . . . and purify [both aorist subjunctive] unto himself a. . . people, zealous of good works." Purity here stresses a separation from iniquity and a devotedness to good works which, if we deny "ungodliness" and "live soberly, righteously and godly in this present world,"would make us his own possession. To be and to remain as Christ's possession is to live in purity, and that purity includes "good works." Without doubt there is an ethical connotation to purity or cleansing. Paul's last word on sanctification in the Pastorals is Titus 3:5. Here Paul says that God saved us "by the washing of regeneration and renewal in the Holy Spirit which he poured out upon us richly through Jesus Christ our Saviour." Since the believer's new life is a recreation and a making new, only divine power can effect it. The Holy Spirit is the agent of this divine work. In concluding this section, although it is evident that the concept of the sanctified life usually expressed in phrases such as "walking in love"; "walking worthy of one's calling"; "walking in newness of life"is absent in the Pastorals, it is nevertheless clear that there exists a close relationship between sanctification as a way of life and the ethical exhortations in the Pastorals.[114]

As stated at the beginning of this chapter, its main purpose is to demonstrate that what was proposed as the understanding of sanctification in Rom. 6-8 is consistent with what one finds on the subject in other parts of the Pauline corpus. This has been done. It has been demonstrated that Paul's understanding of sanctification or holiness in Rom. 6-8 is consistent with his overall view of the Christian life. The people to whom he wrote were people who have entered into a covenant relationship with God through Christ and have made a definite break with the past life of sin. Yet, as Paul often showed, holiness was not only a necessity but a possibility. As Christians who walked in between the times, they were to reflect the image of God to whom they were now related. What one finds in the Pauline corpus provides overwhelming support for the definite ethical implications of the life of sanctification that is to be lived out in holiness in response to the holy God, by the enabling power of the Holy Spirit.

## Conclusion

Two inferences may be drawn from this study. First, although conversion is a genuinely sanctifying divine work, as initial sanctification, it is only the beginning. Second, If lives of holiness were the inevitable result of Christian conversion, much of Paul's writings would not only be unintelligible but also superfluous. Overall, Paul presents holiness both as momentary and progressive. As such, it is wrong to think that a single moment, though necessary and essential, will suffice. The sanctified life admits of growth. Such growth requires the continued cooperation of believers, as the repeated Pauline imperatives suggest. To be holy is to acknowledge and express each day our status as God's holy people. Paul proceeds from the theological assumption that the character of Christians is fundamentally different from that of pagans because of the character of their God. Pagans behave as they do because they "do not know God." Christian holiness involves living "a life worthy of God, who calls you," not only "into his own kingdom and glory" in the future, but to "holiness" in the present (1 Thess. 4:5; 2:12; 4:7).

That God's sanctifying activity affects the Christian's entire being is implied by the Pauline imperatives in Rom. 6:15-23 where Paul exhorts the believers to yield themselves to God. Sanctification can neither be restricted nor reduced to inner motives. It expresses itself in tangible outward behaviour. It would seem to renovate both the character and conduct of believers. It begins in our hearts, but it must eventually emerge in what we do with our hands. It is not restricted to the religious aspects of human life; Paul emphasizes its counter-cultural transformation of all aspects of the ethical life including the sexual behavior of believers. Entire sanctification calls for the complete expression of what it means to be God's holy people.

Sanctification is expected to be a reality in the lives of believers prior to Christ's return. God expects moral integrity of His people, because He has given His Holy Spirit to enable them to live exemplary, Christlike lives in this world as they prepare for the world to come. Thus, it is fair to say that when God transforms the life of a sinner and translates him/her into the state of grace, God frees that sinner from his/her natural bondage under sin. Consequently, one may affirm that where grace reigns and operates, ethical righteousness or holiness follows. The corollary is true: where there is no ethical righteousness, there is no real or true grace, because "grace transforms" (Rom. 5:21).

It is delusional to suggest that a change of status need not be accompanied by a change of state. It must necessarily be. In the same way that sinfulness is both a state and status, holiness must be the same. A dichotomy between the two is simply false. The Christian walk should never be marked by complacency towards sin. After Paul discussed justification by faith and grace in the book of Romans, he emphasized the effect grace has on believers. It has been demonstrated that Paul sets himself apart from present day preachers and scholars who either insist or suggest that Christians may be no different in terms of vital godliness than unbelievers. Such are those who either suggest or teach that Christians may be judicially free from sin, while "fleshly" in the overall tendency of life. Oftentimes, perhaps without realizing it, such teachings do nothing but suggest that sin may still have dominion in the believer's life thus setting up many for tragic self-deception and encouraging spiritual lethargy in others. Grace transforms, and where there is no transformation it is difficult to argue for the presence of grace. Grace will produce change in a person, and if there has been no change, the grace of God has not come upon him. The evidence of grace is a changed heart that brings forth good works (cf. Titus 2:11-14).

# Endnotes

[1] Joel R. Beeke, *God's Call to Sanctification* (Edinburgh: Banner of Truth Trust, 1994), 6.

[2] G. Strecker, "Εὐαγγελίζω," s.v. *Exegetical Dictionary of the New Testament*. Vol. 2. H. Balz and G. Schneider, eds. (Grand Rapids: Eerdmans, 1990), 70.

[3] The phrase literally means "Let it not be." Its force in the argument here is noticeable in the various ways it has been translated e.g. with an idiomatic English statement "God forbid" (KJV), "May it never be" (NASB), "By no means" (RSV), "What a ghastly thought!" (Phillips), "No, no" (NEB).

[4] Manfred T. Brauch, *Hard Sayings of Paul* (Downer's Grove: InterVarsity, 1989), 39.

[5] Cf. C. A. A. Scott, *Christianity according to St. Paul* (Cambridge: Cambridge University, 1932), 162. "The important thing is to note at how many points the symbol corresponds to the thing symbolized."

[6] Douglas Moo, *Romans 1-8*. Wycliffe Exegetical Commentary (Chicago: Moody Press, 1991), *Romans*, 376. Other scholars agree with this position. Among such are: C. K. Barrett, *A Commentary on the Epistle to the Romans* (New York: Harper & Row, 1974), 122; C. E. B. Cranfield, *A Critical and Exegetical Commentary on the Epistle to the Romans*. The International Critical Commentary (Edinburgh: T & T Clark, 1979), 301; Leon Morris, *Romans* (Grand Rapids: Eerdmans), 247.

[7] Moo, *Romans 1-8*, 382-83: "The compartmentalizing of Paul's 'juridical' and 'participationist' language cannot be done, and any explanation of the role of baptism in Romans 6 must come to grips with the obvious centrality of faith as the means by which our relationship to Christ is appropriated."

[8] Richard B. Gaffin, Jr., *Resurrection and Redemption: A Study in Paul's Soteriology*, 2nd ed. (Phillipsburg: Presbyterian and Reformed, 1987), 47. He also rightly concludes: "If only the former [*solidarity*] were the case, Paul would be arguing directly from the once-for-all event of Christ's resurrection to the believer's new walk, and this would involve an hiatus completely foreign to the controlling interest and structure of the thought in the immediate and broader context (6:1-7:6). Paul's repeated stress is that death with Christ (to sin and to the law) includes an experiential aspect which excludes the possibility of continuing in the bondage and practice of sin. Accordingly, resurrection with Christ likewise involves an existential component."

[9] Murray, *The Epistle to the Romans*. NICNT (Grand Rapids: Eerdmans, 1968, 1990), 218. Paul here uses the word σύμφυτοι to express the believer's union with Christ. The word means "grown together" (BAGD). It is generally agreed that the word derives from συμφύω, "make to grow together," rather than συμφυτεύω, "plant together" and it signifies a growing together. Cf. Godet, *Romans*, 242 says that this adjective "denotes the organic union in virtue of which one being shares the life, growth and phases of existence belonging to another".

[10] τοῦτο γινώυκοντες ὅτι may be taken as an allusion to some experimental knowledge that the Christians had which Paul was now referring to as a confirmation of what he had just stated, thus taking the participle in a causal sense (see A. T. Robertson, *A Grammar of The Greek New Testament in the Light of Historical Research* [Nashville: Broadman, 1934], 1128), or as the start of a new paragraph, in which case Paul was about to introduce some new facts that are relevant to his argument.

[11] See, Richard R. Melick, Jr., *Philippians, Colossians, Philemon*, The New American Commentary (Nashville: Broadman, 1991), 295.

[12] This is well stated by J. R. W. Stott, "The 'old self' denotes, not our old unregenerate nature, but our old unregenerate life...'the man we once were'.... So what was crucified with Christ was not part of me called my old nature, but the whole of me as I was before I was converted," *Men Made New: An Exposition of Romans 5-8* (London: Inter Varsity, 1966), 45; Cf.Murray, *Romans*, 219; Cf. Cranfield, *Romans*, 309.

[13] Hermann Ridderbos, *Paul: An Outline of His Theology.* John R. De Witt, trans. (Grand Rapids: Eerdmans, 1975), 62ff. He maintains that the contrast between the old and new man is to be understood, "not in the sense of the *ordo salutis*, but in that of the history of redemption;... not first of all in a personal and ethical sense, but in a redemptive-historical, eschatological sense." Ridderbos is correct in his observation that the old and new man is not about ordo salutis. However, his stripping the concepts of their ethical nuance does injustice to the entire passage. As I have tried to show above in my discussion of other concepts, in v. 6, as in this context as a whole, Paul's primary emphasis is on that radical transformation and new situation of faith-union effected in the life history of the believer.

[14] Thayer interprets "our old self"..."as we were before, our mode of thought, feeling, action, had been changed." Cf. Joseph H. Thayer, *A Greek-English Lexicon of the New Testament* (New York: American Book Co, 1886), 474. Cremer states that the term "old self" "designates a particular mode or manifestation of human nature... human nature... as the individual is naturally." Cf. Hermann Cremer,

# Endnotes

*Biblio-Theological Lexicon of New Testament Greek*, trans. William Urwick (Edinburgh: T. and T. Clark, 1962), 105. Ardnt and Gingrich use the term to indicate the earlier, unregenerate man. Cf. BAGD, 610.

[15] Robertson, *Grammar*, 915, while recognizing that the indicatives do not necessarily guarantee the *reality* of a thing nevertheless state the thing as *true*. "Actuality is implied, to be sure but nothing more."

[16] Richard E. Howard, *Newness of Life: A Study in the Thought of Paul* (Kansas City: Beacon Hill Press, 1975), 102.

[17] Howard, *Newness of Life*, 102. His observation is quite helpful. He states, "When a rigid theological interpretation is superimposed on a term or concept with no regard to the context or its meaning elsewhere, the result is an invalid biblical hermeneutic that destroys scriptural authority."

[18] Frederick Godet, *Romans* (Grand Rapids: Kregel Publications, 1977), 245.

[19] D. E. H. Whiteley, *The Theology of St. Paul* (Oxford: Basil Blackwell, 1964), 42

[20] Cf. Moo, *Romans 1-8*, 395. For other views about this verse, particularly on the use of the terminology of sanctification, see, Bruce, *Romans*, 131; Murray, *Romans*, 222.

[21] Cf. Roger Bowen, *A Guide to Romans* (Quezon City: New Day Publishers, 1997) 85.

[22] On the one hand, it is recognised that the aorist denotes simple action, emphasizing the act itself. As such it often conveys the sense of a momentary, even a one-time act. Nevertheless, on the other hand, the momentary sense of the aorist does not preclude or deny the possibility of a continuing action. For example, in the so-called Ingressive Aorist, the tense is used to indicate the beginning action of a sequence or process. As such, context must decide the issue.

[23] C. H. Dodd, *The Epistle to the Romans*. The Moffatt New Testament Commentary (New York: Harper and Brothers, 1932), 98. Dodd's critical question, "Would not that 'slavery to righteousness', more aptly describe life under the Law than the condition of Christian freedom?" is in this context to be emphatically answered in the negative.

[24] Paul is aware that the figure of slavery is unworthy, inadequate and apt to be grievously misleading, as a way of indicating the believers' relation to God (see v. 19a). But he found this to be the best human illustration possible to communicate total commitment, total belonging-ness, total responsibility and total accountability" to God in our life of grace.

[25] "Themselves" is used to reflect the term *mél ¯e* by which Paul refers to the Romans in this context. They gave "their members" to sin. Cf. 1 Cor. 12.20f.,

24-26. In Paul the members are not under autonomous control but responsible to God. Here in Rom. 6.19 Paul is saying it was the whole person who was the slave of sin (cf. Rom. 6.13 and Paul's alternation from *ta mélē* to *heautous* to *ta mélē*).

[26] David Peterson, *Possessed by God: A New Testament theology of sanctification and holiness* (Leicester, England: Apollos, 1995), 142.

[27] A. T. Robertson, *Word Pictures of the New Testament* (Nashville: Broadman Press, 1932, 33), 4: 365.

[28] James Denney "St. Paul's Epistle to the Romans," *The Expositor's Greek New Testament,* vol.2 (Grand Rapids: Eerdmans, 1988 repr.), 2: 636.

[29] Cf. Denney, "Romans," 234 n. 21; H. A. W. Meyer, *The Epistle to the Romans*, MeyerK. 2 vols, repr. (Edinburgh: T & T Clark, 1881,1884), 1:311.

[30] Ibid., 636.

[31] James Fraser, *A Treatise on Sanctification* (Audubon, NJ: Old Path Publications, 1992).

[32] Sinclair Ferguson's foreword comments in James Fraser, *A Treatise on Sanctification*, iv.

[33] For a detailed study of the passage including an exhaustive bibliography, see Michael Paul Middendorf, *The "I" in the Storm* (St. Louis, Missouri: Concordia Press, 1997).

[34] Murray, *Romans*, 239.

[35] Robert C. Tannehill, *Dying and Rising with Christ: A Study in Pauline Theology* (Berlin: Topplemann, 1967), 43.

[36] A. J. M Wedderburn,. "Hellenistic Christian Traditions in Romans 6?" *New Testament Studies* 29 (1982), 338.

[37] Literally means "to be lord or master," "rule," "lord it (over)," "control," "reign."

[38] There is no consensus of opinion with regards to what the righteousness of God means. In my opinion the righteousness of God is not only imputed but imparted.

[39] More will be said on the "flesh" in the discussion on Rom. 8 in the next chapter.

[40] One of the most important and yet confusing areas in the writings of Paul is his teaching on the law. Despite the volumes that have been written, as well as the vast amount of effort that has been put into the study of this area of Pauline theology, no consensus exists either on methodology or results. This is well stated by Snodgrass: "Presuppositional and methodological differences are magnified to such an extent by ecclesiastical traditions and existential concerns that what Paul actually said is difficult to determine." Cf. Klyne Snodgrass, "Spheres of influence as a possible solution to the problem of Paul and the Law," *JSNT* 32 (1988): 93-113.

# Endnotes

41 So Richard N. Longenecker, *Galatians*, Word Biblical Commentary (Dallas: Word Books, 1990), 91; Tannehill, *Dying and Rising*, 55.

42 Contra Tannehill, *Dying and Rising*, 56.

43 Tannehill, *Dying and Rising*, 57.

44 Donald.Guthrie, New Testament Theology. (England: Inter-Varsity, 1981), 646.

45 J. G. D Dunn, *Romans 1-8*, Word Biblical Commentary. (Dallas: Word Books, 1988), 359.

46 Moo, *Romans 1-8*, 437. He has rightly described this interpretation "minimalist," seeing it as an extreme reaction against the allegorical interpretation. The minimalist approach robs the details of the illustration of any significant value.

47 Stanley K. Stowers, *A Rereading of Romans: Justice, Jews, and Gentiles* (New Haven: Yale University Press, 1994), 258-269.

48 Thanks to Dean Flemming for pointing my attention to the fact that the trend in scholarship in recent decades seems has been away from equating the two.

49 Scholars differ in opinion whether the section should comprise of chapters 5-8 (so C.E.B. Cranfield, *Romans*, Vol. 1., ICC [Edingburgh: T. & T. Clark, 1975]; Douglas Moo, *Romans 1-8*; Dunn *Romans 1-8*, Gordon Fee, *God's Empowering Presence: The Holy Spirit in the Letters of Paul* [Peabody: Hendrickson Publishers, 1994], 499). This writer takes the latter view.

50 F. Godet, *Commentary on St. Paul's Epistle to the Romans* (Grand Rapids: Zondervan, 1969), 295 quotes Spener as saying that "if the holy Scripture was a ring, and the Epistle to the Romans its precious stone, chapter 8 would be the sparkling point of the jewel."

51 Kaylor, *Paul's Covenant Community*, 141-142.

52 Cf. Fee, *God's Empowering Presence*, 517 comments on Rom 5:1-8:39: ". . .nonetheless the Spirit is the experiential key to the whole: God in love is creating a people for his name, apart from the Law . . . . All of this is actualized in the church (and in the believer as well, of course) by the Spirit whom God has given."

53 Cf. Howard, *Newness of Life*, 160

54 Fee, *God's Empowering Presence*, 516, 517.

55 Rom. 7:6 is the essential presupposition of Rom. 8, for it is clear that the perspective of faith that Paul develops in Rom. 8 was already the foundation of his argument in Rom. 7.

56 Roger Bowen, *A Guide to Romans* (Quezon City, Philippines: New Day Publishers, 1997), 102.

[57] Adam Clarke, "Romans" in *Clarke's Commentary: Matthew-Revelation* (Nashville: Abingdon, n.d), 93.

[58] Denney, "Romans," 644.

[59] Kaylor, *Paul's Covenant Community*, 150.

[60] Cf. Clifton J. Allen, *The Gospel According to Paul: A Study of the Letter to the Romans* (Nashville: Convention Press, 1958), 88.

[61] Contra Kaylor, *Paul's Covenant Community*, 144.

[62] Howard, *Newness of Life*, 163.

[63] John Wesley, *Explanatory Notes on the New Testament* (London: Epworth Press, 1950 repr.), 547.

[64] William G. Greathouse, *The Epistle to the Romans* (Kansas City: Beacon Hill Press, 1980), 169.

[65] Udo Schnelle, *The Human Condition*, O.C. Dean Jr., trans. (Minneapolis: Fortress Press, 1996), 61.

[66] Contra Fee, *God's Empowering Presence*, 543n.213 who maintains an individualistic interpretation.

[67] Trevor J. Burke, "Adoption and the Spirit in Romans 8," *EQ* 70/4 (1998), 311-324.

[68] Leon Morris, *The Epistle to the Romans* (Leicester: InterVarsity Press, 1988), 311.

[69] Thus γάρ in verse 13 is to be taken as explanatory rather than causal.

[70] E. Kasemann, *Romans*, 226 and Dunn, *Romans*, 450.

[71] Burke notes that BAGD does not include 'drive' as a possible meaning for the verb ἄγω (*ago*). Rather it has the passage under 'be led/allowed oneself to be led' which is very different to 'be driven.'

[72] Although it may not be altogether excluded.

[73] William Hendriksen, *Commentary on the Epistle to the Romans* (Grand Rapids: Baker Book House, 1981), 256.

[74] Sinclair B. Ferguson, *The Christian Life: A Doctrinal Introduction* (Edinburgh: Banner of Truth Trust, 1981), 100.

[75] Schreiner, *Romans*, 423.

[76] For a comprehensive treatment on the subject of adoption in Paul, see James M. Scott, *Adoption as Sons of God. An Exegetical Investigation into the Background of ΥΙΟΘΕΣΙΑ in the Pauline Corpus*. WUNT 2/48. Tübingen: Paul Siebeck, 1992.

[77] It remains a matter of scholarly debate how συμμαρτυρεῖ τῷ πνεύματι ἡμῶν is to be understood. Does the Spirit testify with or to our spirit that we are the children of God? Scholars differ in opinion. For a detailed discussion, see Daniel Wallace, *Greek Grammar Beyond the Basics: An Exegetical Syntax of the New Testament* (Grand Rapids: Zondervan Publishing House, 1996), 160-161.

# Endnotes

[78] L. H. Marshall, *The Ethics of the New Testament* (London: MacMillan, 1960), 259.

[79] Willam Greathouse, *Wholeness in Christ: Toward A Biblical Theology of Holiness* (Kansas City: Beacon Hill Press, 1998), 120.

[80] Kaylor, *Paul's Covenant Community*, 153.

[81] Ibid., 155.

[82] One cannot but notice Paul's juxtapostion of the individual and the community here. He speaks of our adoption as sons (plural) and the redemption of our body (singular).

[83] It also appears in several important passages in the Pauline corpus, among which are Rom. 1:23; 1 Cor. 11:7; 2 Cor. 4:3; Col. 3:10.

[84] Allen, *Gospel According to Paul*, 95-96.

[85] Bowens, *A Guide to Romans*, 118.

[86] Rom. 6:15-23; Phil. 2:13; Col. 3:5, etc.

[87] Instead of "your members" in 6:13, Paul employs "your bodies" in 12:2. However, both are essentially the same.

[88] Richard B. Hays, *The Moral Vision of the New Testament* (San Francisco: Harper Collins Publishers, 1996), 196-197.

[89] Bence, *Romans*, 218.

[90] Please see also by this author, *Holiness and Community in 2 Cor. 6:14-7:1: Paul's view of Communal Holiness in the Corinthian Correspondence* (New York: Peter Lang, 2001) for a detailed study of holiness in the Corinthian correspondence.

[91] Adewuya, *Holiness and Community*, 134.

[92] Ibid.

[93] Furnish, *2 Corinthians*, 499.

[94] Murphy-O'Connor, *Theology of 2 Corinthians* (Cambridge: Cambridge University Press, 1991), 108.

[95] A. Andrew Das, "Oneness in Christ: The *Nexus Indivulsus* Between Justification and Sanctification in Paul's Letter to the Galatians," *Concordia Journal* 21/2 (April 1995), 2-3.

[96] Longenecker is probably right in his observation that, "the aorist verb..., since it identifies the crucifixion of the flesh in the believer's experience as being a past event but assigns that event to no specific time in the past is best translated as a perfect, 'they have crucified'." Cf. *Galatians*, 264.

[97] So G. E Ladd, *A Theology of the New Testament* (Grand Rapids: Eerdmans, 1974), 485.

[98] In my view, by interpreting it this way, both the force of the active voice as well as the distinctive Pauline usage of the metaphor are preserved. While on the one

hand the temptation of forcing a juridical interpretation is avoided, on the other it clearly goes against the view that crucifixion in this verse is a reference to a continuous self-denial, a daily carrying of the cross, a usage that is more noticeable in the Gospels.

99 In this view, Gal. 5:24 is "simply emphasising that the 'passions' with their basis the 'flesh' are crucified and overcome in Christians; this has taken place in baptism." Cf. Wilhelm Michaelis, S.v. "πάθημα" *Theological Dictionary of the New Testament*. Eds. Kittel, G. and G. Friedrich.G. W. Bromiley, trans. (Grand Rapids: Eerdmans,1971), 5:930-931.

100 J. Schneider, s.v. "σταυρόω" *Theological Dictionary of the New Testament*. Eds. Kittel, G. and G. Friedrich. G. W. Bromiley, trans. (Grand Rapids: Eerdmans, 1971), 7:583-4.

101 Michael Parsons, "Being Precedes Act: Indicative and Imperative in Paul's Writing," *Evangelical Quarterly* 88/2 (1988), 122.

102 Parsons, "Indicatives and Imperatives," 119.

103 Olive M. Winchester and Ross E. Price, *Crisis Experiences in the New Testament* (Kansas City: Beacon Hill Press, 1953), 71.

104 George Allen Turner, *The Vision Which Transforms* (Kansas City: Beacon Hill Press, 1964), 88.

105 Walters, *Perfection in New Testament Theology* (Lewiston, NY.: Edwin Mellen Press, 1995), 214.

106 Marvin R. Vincent, *Epistles to the Philippians and to Philemon*, ICC (Edinburgh: T & T Clark, 1897), 57.

107 Ibid., 8.

108 Howard, *Newness*, 191.

109 Walters, *Perfection*, 215.

110 So also in Rom. 1:27; 2:9; 4:5; 5:3; 2 Cor. 4:17; 5:5; 8:11; 11:11; 12:12; Eph. 6:13.

111 G. Hawthorne, *Philippians*, Word Biblical Themes (Waco: Word Books, 1987), 94.

112 Having weighed the available evidence, I conclude there is more in favour of Paul's authorship of the Pastorals.

113 Daniel Spross, "Holiness in the Pastorals," *Biblical Resources for Holiness Preaching*, H. Ray Dunning and Neil B. Wiseman, eds. (Kansas City: Beacon Hill Press, 1990), 214.

114 Spross, "Holiness in the Pastorals," 223.

# Bibliography
(Works Consulted)

## A. COMMENTARIES

Allen, Clifton J. *The Gospel According to Paul: A Study of the Letter to the Romans.* Nashville: Convention Press, 1958.

Barrett, C. K. *A Commentary on the Epistle to the Romans.* New York: Harper & Row, 1974.

Beeke, Joel R.. *God's Call to Sanctification.* Edinburgh: Banner of Truth Trust, 1994.

Bowen, Roger. *A Guide to Romans.* Quezon City: New Day Publishers, 1997.

Bruce, F. F. *Romans.* Tyndale New Testament Commentaries. Revised Edition. Grand Rapids: Eerdmans, 1985.

Clarke, Adam. "Romans." In Clarke's Commentary, Matthew-Revelation. Nashville: Abingdon, n.d.

Cranfield, C. E. B. *A Critical and Exegetical Commentary on the Epistle to the Romans.* The International Critical Commentary. Edinburgh: T & T Clark, 1979.

Denney, James."Saint Paul's Epistle to the Romans." *The Expositor's Greek Testament.* Ed. W. Robertson Nicoll. Reprint. Grand Rapids: Eerdmans, 1988.

Dodd, C. H. *The Epistle to the Romans.* The Moffatt New Testament Commentary. New York: Harper and Brothers, 1932.

Dunn, J. G. D. *Romans 1-8, Romans 9-16.* Word Biblical Commentary. Dallas: Word Books, 1988.

Edwards, James R. *Romans.* New International Bible Commentary. Peabody: Hendrickson, 1992.

Fitzmyer, Joseph. "The Letter to the Romans." *The New Jerome Biblical Commentary.* Eds. Brown, Raymond E., Joseph A. Fitzmyer, and Roland E. Murphy. Englewood Cliffs: Prentice Hall, 1990.

Godet, Frederick L. *Romans.* Grand Rapids: Kregel, 1977.

Greathouse, William, M. *The Epistle to the Romans*. Beacon Bible Commentary. Kansas City: Beacon Hill, 1980.

G. Hawthorne, *Philippians*. Word Biblical Themes. Waco: Word Books, 1987.

Kasemann, Ernst. *Commentary on Romans*. Translated and edited by G. W. Bromiley. Grand Rapids: Eerdmans, 1980.

Knox, John. "The Epistle to the Romans," *Interpreter's Bible*, vol. 9. New York: Abingdon, 1954.

Lagrange, M. J. *Saint Paul: Epitre aux Romains*. Etudes Bibliques. Paris: Gabalda, 1950.

Leenhardt, Franz J. *The Epistle to the Romans*. English Translation. London: Lutterworth, 1961.

Lenski, R. C. H. *St. Paul's Epistle to the Romans*. Minneapolis: Augsburg, 1945.

Longenecker, Richard N. *Galatians*. Word Biblical Commentary. Dallas: Word Books, 1990.

Meyer, H. A. W. *The Epistle to the Romans*, MeyerK. 2 vols. 1872. Reprint. Edinburgh: T & T Clark, 1881,1884.

Moo, Douglas. *Romans 1-8*. Wycliffe Exegetical Commentary. Chicago: Moody, 1991.

Morris, Leon. *Romans*. Grand Rapids: Eerdmans, 1988.

Murphy-O'Connor, Jerome. "The Second letter to the Corinthians." *The New Jerome Biblical Commentary*. Eds. Brown, Raymond E., Joseph A. Fitzmyer, and Roland E. Murphy. Englewood Cliffs: Prentice Hall, 1990.

Murray, John. *The Epistle to the Romans*. New International Commentary on the New Testament. Grand Rapids: Eerdmans, 1968, 1990.

Nygren, Anders. *Commentary on Romans*. Translated by Carl C. Rasmussen. Philadelphia: Fortress, 1949.

Sanday, W. and Headlam, A. C. *The Epistle to the Romans*. The International Critical Commentary. Edinburgh: T & T Clark, 1905.

Ziesler, John. *Paul's Letter to the Romans*. Trinity Press International New Testament Commentaries. London: SCM, 1989.

## B. PAULINE STUDIES

Bornkamm, Gunther. *Paul*. Translated by M. G. Stalker. New York: Harper and Row, 1971.

___. 'The Revelation of Christ to Paul on the Damascus Road and Paul's Doctrine of Justification and Revelation. A Study in Galatians 1.' In *Reconciliation and Hope*. New Testament Essays on Atonement and Eschatology Presented to L. L. Morris. Ed. R. J. Banks. Exeter: Paternoster, 1974.

Bouttier, Michel. *Christianity According to Paul*. Translated by Frank Clarke. London: SCM, 1966.

Brauch, Manfred T. *Hard Sayings of Paul*. Downers Grove: InterVarsity, 1989.

Bruce, F. F. *Paul and Jesus*. Grand Rapids: Baker, 1974.

___. *Paul, Apostle of the Heart Set Free*. Grand Rapids: Eerdmans, 1977.

Deissmann, Adolf. *Paul: A Study in Social and Religious History*. Translated by W. E. Wilson. New York: Harper and Row, 1926, 1957.

Dupont, J. "The Conversion of Paul, and its Influence on his Understanding of Salvation by Faith." *Apostolic History and the Gospel: Biblical and Historical Essays presented to F. F. Bruce*. Eds. W. W. Gasque and R. P. Martin. Exeter: Paternoster, 1970.

Ellis, E. Earle. *Paul and His Recent Interpreters*. Grand Rapids: Eerdmans, 1961.

Fee, Gordon. *God's Empowering Presence: The Holy Spirit in the Letters of Paul*. Peabody: Hendrickson Publishers, 1994.

Fitzmyer, Joseph A. "Pauline Theology," *New Jerome Biblical Commentary*. Eds. Raymond E. Brown, Joseph A. Fitzmyer, and Roland E. Murphy. Englewood Cliffs: Prentice Hall, 1990.Furnish, V. P. *Theology and Ethics in Paul*. Nashville: Abingdon, 1981.

Gaffin, Richard B. *Resurrection and Redemption: A Study in Paul's Soteriology*. Phillipsburg: Presbyterian and Reformed, 1987.

Howard Richard E. *Newness of Life: A Study in the Thought of Paul*. Kansas City: Beacon Hill, 1975.

Hubner, Hans. *Law in Paul's Thought*. Translated by James C. G. Greig. Edinburgh: T & T Clark, 1984.

Kasemann, Ernst. *Perspectives on Paul*. Translated by Margaret Kohl. Philadelphia: Fortress, 1971.

Kennedy, H. A. A. *The Theology of the Epistles*. Edinburgh: University Press, 1919.

Kim, S. *The Origin of Paul's Gospel*. Tübingen: Mohr, 1981.

Manson, T. W. *On Paul and Jesus.* Ed. M. Black London: SCM, 1963.

Martin, Ralph P. *Reconciliation: A Study of Paul's Theology.* Grand Rapids: Zondervan, 1989.

Middendorf, Michael Paul *The "I" in the Storm.* St. Louis, Missouri: Concordia Press, 1997.

Peterson, David. *Possessed by God: A New Testament theology of sanctification and holiness.* Leicester, England: Apollos, 1995.

Quek, Swee-hwa. "Adam and Christ According to Paul" In *Pauline Studies: Essays Presented to F. F. Bruce on His 70th Birthday.* Eds. Hagner, Donald A. and J. Harris Murray. Grand Rapids: Eerdmans, 1980.

Ridderbos, Hermann. *Paul: An Outline of His Theology.* Translated by John R. De Witt. Grand Rapids: Eerdmans, 1975.

Robinson, H. W. *Corporate Personality in Ancient Israel.* Facet Books, Biblical Series, 11. Ed. J. Reumann. Philadelphia: Fortress, 1964.

Schnelle, Udo. *The Human Condition.* Translated by O.C. Dean Jr. Minneapolis: Fortress Press, 1996.

Schweizer, Albert. *Paul and His Intepreters.* Translated by W. Montgomery. New York: Schoken, 1912, 1964.

Scott, James M. *Adoption as Sons of God. An Exegetical Investigation into the Background of* ΥΙΟΘΕΣΙΑ *in the Pauline Corpus.* WUNT 2/48. Tübingen: Paul Siebeck, 1992.

Shedd, R. P. *Man in Community.* Grand Rapids: Eerdmans, 1964.

Stacey, W. D. *The Pauline View of Man.* New York: St. Martin's, 1956.

Stendahl, K. *Paul among Jews and Gentiles.* Philadelphia: Fortress, 1977.

Tannehill, Robert C. *Dying and Rising with Christ: A Study in Pauline Theology.* Berlin: Topplemann, 1967. Whiteley, D. E. H. *The Theology of St Paul.* Oxford: Blackwell, 1964.

## C. OTHER WORKS

Barclay, William. *Flesh and Spirit.* Grand Rapids: Baker, 1976.

Barr, James. *The Semantics of Biblical Language.* London: SCM, 1983.

Barth, K. "Rudolf Bultmann- An Attempt to Understand Him." In *Kerygma and Myth.* Ed. Hans-Werner Bartsch. London: SPCK, 1962.

Beasley-Murray, G. R. *Baptism in the New Testament.* London: Macmillan, 1962.

Best, E. *One Body in Christ.* London: SPCK, 1965.

# Bibliography

Bultmann, Rudolf. *Theology of the New Testament*. Translated by Kendrick Grobel. New York: Charles Scribner, 1955.

___. *Existence and Faith*. Translated by S. M. Ogden. Cleveland: World, 1960.

Conzelmann, Hans. *An Outline of the Theology of the New Testament*. Translated by John Bowden. London: SCM, 1969.

Corbett, P. E. *The Roman Law of Marriage*. Reprint. Oxford: Clarendon, 1969.

Cremer, Hermann. *Biblio-Theological Lexicon of New Testament Greek*. Translated by William Urwick. Edinburgh: T. & T. Clark, 1962.

Daube, D. "Participle and Imperative in 1 Peter." In E. G. Selwyn. *The First Epistle of Peter*. London: Macmillan, 1947.

Dunn, J. D. G. *Baptism in The Holy Spirit*. London: SCM Press, 1971.

Ervin, Howard M. *Conversion-Initiation and The Baptism in the Holy Spirit*. Peabody, Massachusetts: Hendrickson, 1984.

Ferguson, Sinclair B. *The Christian Life: A Doctrinal Introduction* (Edinburgh: Banner of Truth Trust, 1981.

Fraser, James *A Treatise on Sanctification*. Audubon, NJ: Old Path Publications, 1992.

Gemeren Van, W. A. "Solidarity of the Race." *Evangelical Dictionary of Theology*. Ed. Walter A. Elwell. Grand Rapids: Baker, 1984.

Goppelt, Leonhard. *Theology of the New Testament*. Translated by John E. Asup. Grand Rapids: Eerdmans, 1982.

Greathouse, Willam. *Wholeness in Christ: Toward A Biblical Theology of Holiness* (Kansas City: Beacon Hill Press, 1998.

Gundry, Robert. *Soma in Biblical Theology*. Cambridge: Cambridge University Press, 1976.

Guthrie, Donald. *New Testament Theology*. England: Inter-Varsity, 1981.

Harrisville, Roy. *The Concept of Newness in the New Testament*. Minneapolis: Augsburg, 1960.

Hasel, Gerhard F. *New Testament Theology: Basic Issues in the Current Debate*. Grand Rapids: Eerdmans, 1978.

Kümmel, W. G. *The New Testament: The History of the Investigation of Its Problems*. Translated by S. Mclean Gilmour and Howard C. Kee. Nashville: Abingdon, 1972.

___. *The Theology of the New Testament according to Its Major Witnesses*. Nashville & New York: Abingdon, 1973.

Ladd, G. E. *A Theology of the New Testament*. Grand Rapids: Eerdmans, 1974.

Longenecker, Richard. *The Ministry and Message of Paul*. Grand Rapids: Baker, 1971.

Macquarrie, John. *Studies in Christian Existentialism*. Philadelphia: Westminster, 1965.

Marshall, L. H. *The Ethics of the New Testament*. London: MacMillan, 1960..

Mascall, E. L. *Christ, the Christian, and the Church*. London: Longmans, 1940.

Meeks, W. A. *The First Urban Christians*. New Haven: Yale University Press, 1983.

Michaelis, Wilhelm. S.v. "πάθημα" *Theological Dictionary of the New Testament*. Eds. Kittel, G. and G. Friedrich. Translated by G. W. Bromiley. 10 vols. Grand Rapids: Eerdmans. ET 1964-1978.

Nielson, John B. *In Christ*. Kansas City: Beacon Hill, 1960.

Oepke, Albrecht. S.v. "ἐν." *Theological Dictionary of the New Testament*. Eds. Kittel, G. and G. Friedrich. Translated by Bromiley, G. W. 10 vols. Grand Rapids: Eerdmans. ET 1964-1978.

Purkiser, W. *Sanctification and Its Synonyms*. Kansas City: Beacon Hill, 1961.

Robertson, A. T. *A Grammar of the Greek New Testament in the light of Historical Research*. Nashville: Broadman, 1934.

Schneider, J. S.v. "σταυρόω" *Theological Dictionary of the New Testament*. Eds. Kittel, G. and G. Friedrich. Translated by G. W. Bromiley. 10 vols. Grand Rapids: Eerdmans. ET 1964-1978.

Schrenk, G. S. v. "δικαιόω." *Theological Dictionary of the New Testament*. Eds. Kittel, G. and G. Friedrich. Translated by G. W. Bromiley. 10 vols. Grand Rapids: Eerdmans. ET 1964-1978.

Scott, C. A. A. *Christianity according to St Paul*. Cambridge: Cambridge University Press, 1932.

Smedes, Lewis B. *Union with Christ*. Grand Rapids: Eerdmans, 1983.

Spross, Daniel. "Holiness in the Pastorals." In *Biblical Resources for Holiness Preaching*. Dunning H. Ray and Neil B. Wiseman, eds. (Kansas City: Beacon Hill Press, 1990)

Stewart, James. *A Man in Christ*. New York: Harper and Row, 1935.

# Bibliography

Stott, J. R. W. *Men Made New: An Exposition of Romans 5-8*. Grand Rapids: Baker, 1966.

_____. *Essential Freedom*. England: Inter-Varsity, 1988.

Thayer, Joseph H. *A Greek-English Lexicon of the New Testament*. New York: American Book, 1886.

Trench, R. C. *Synonyms of the New Testament*. Reprint. Grand Rapids: Eerdman's, 1969.

Warfield, B. B.*Studies in Theology*. Edingburgh: Banner of Truth, 1988.

## D. JOURNAL ARTICLES

Black II, C. C., "Pauline Perspectives on Death in Romans 5-8." *Journal of Biblical Literature* 103/3 (1984): 413-433.

Black, M. "The Pauline Doctrine of Second Adam." *Scottish Journal of Theology* 7 (1954): 170-179.

Brendan Bryne, S.J., "Living out the Righteousness of God: The Contribution of Rom. 6:1-8:13 to an Understanding of Paul's Ethical Presuppositions." *Catholic Bible Quarterly* 43 (1981): 557-581.

Burke, Trevor J. "Adoption and the Spirit in Romans 8." *EQ* 70/4 (1998), 311-324.

Dennison, William D. "Indicative and Imperative: The Basic Structure of Pauline Ethics." *Calvin Theological Journal* 14/1 (1979): 55-78.

Keck, Leander E. "Jesus in Romans." *Journal of Biblical Literature* 108/3 (1989): 443-460.

Little, Joyce A. "Paul's Use of Analogy: A Structural Analysis of Romans 7:1-6." *Catholic Bible Quarterly* 46 (1984): 76-92.

Murray, John. "Definitive Santification." *Calvin Theological Journal* 2/1 (1967): 5-21.

Neugebauer, F. "Das paulininische 'In Christo'." *New Testament Sudies* 4 (1957-58): 124-138.

Parsons, Michael. "Being Precedes Act: Indicative and Imperative in Paul's Writing," *Evangelical Quarterly* 88/2 (1988):99-127.

Snodgrass, Klyne. "Sphere of Influence: A Possible Solution to the Problem of Paul and the Law." *Journal for the Studies of the New Testament* 32 (1988): 93-113.

Strecker, Georg. "Indicative and Imperative according to Paul." *Australian Biblical Review* 35 (1987): 60-72.

Wedderburn, A. J. M. "Some Observations on Paul's Use of the Phrases 'in Christ' and 'with Christ'." *Journal for the Studies of the New Testament* 25 (1985): 83-97.

Wedderburn, A. J. M. "Hellenistic Christian Traditions in Romans 6?" *New Testament Studies* 29 (1982): 337-355.

Yates, Roy. "The Christian Way of Life: The Parenetic Material in Colossians 3:1-4:6." *Evangelical Quarterly* 63/3 (1991): 241-251.